T0316601

.

Cambridge Elements ≡

Elements in Histories of Emotions and the Senses
edited by
Jan Plamper
University of Limerick

FEELING TERRIFIED?

The Emotions of Online Violent Extremism

Lise Waldek
Macquarie University, Sydney

Julian Droogan
Macquarie University, Sydney

Catharine Lumby
University of Sydney

CAMBRIDGE
UNIVERSITY PRESS

CAMBRIDGE
UNIVERSITY PRESS

University Printing House, Cambridge CB2 8BS, United Kingdom

One Liberty Plaza, 20th Floor, New York, NY 10006, USA

477 Williamstown Road, Port Melbourne, VIC 3207, Australia

314–321, 3rd Floor, Plot 3, Splendor Forum, Jasola District Centre,
New Delhi – 110025, India

103 Penang Road, #05–06/07, Visioncrest Commercial, Singapore 238467

Cambridge University Press is part of the University of Cambridge.

It furthers the University's mission by disseminating knowledge in the pursuit of
education, learning, and research at the highest international levels of excellence.

www.cambridge.org
Information on this title: www.cambridge.org/9781108814232
DOI: 10.1017/9781108886369

First published 2021

A catalogue record for this publication is available from the British Library.

ISBN 978-1-108-81423-2 Paperback
ISSN 2632-1068 (online)
ISSN 2632-105X (print)

Feeling Terrified?

The Emotions of Online Violent Extremism

Elements in Histories of Emotions and the Senses

DOI: 10.1017/9781108886369
First published online: November 2021

Lise Waldek
Macquarie University, Sydney

Julian Droogan
Macquarie University, Sydney

Catharine Lumby
University of Sydney

Author for correspondence: Lise Waldek, Lise.waldek@mq.edu.au

Abstract: This Element presents original research into how young people interact with violent extremist material, including terrorist propaganda, when online. It explores a series of emotional and behavioural responses that challenge assumptions that terror or trauma are the primary emotional responses to these online environments. It situates young people's emotional responses within a social framework, revealing them to have a relatively sophisticated relationship with violent extremism on social media that challenges simplistic concerns about processes of radicalisation. The Element draws on four years of research, including quantitative surveys and qualitative focus groups with young people, and presents a unique perspective drawn from young people's experiences.

Keywords: violent extremism, emotions, social media, youth, resilience

ISBNs: 9781108814232 (PB), 9781108886369 (OC)
ISSNs: 2632-1068 (online), 2632-105X (print)

Contents

1 Introduction

One autumn Friday in 2019 shortly after lunchtime, an Australian man Brenton Tarrant strapped a camera to his helmet, linked the feed to Facebook Live, and went on to carry out New Zealand's worst-ever terrorist attack. Inspired by far-right Islamophobia and white supremacism, the livestreamed attack eventually claimed the lives of fifty-one adults and children attending two mosques in the city of Christchurch, while leaving a further forty injured. Friday, March 15 became, in the words of Prime Minister Jacinda Ardern, "one of New Zealand's darkest days" and the perpetrator became New Zealand's first convicted terrorist. That day made history in another sense. The Christchurch attack, as it came to be known, was not the first terrorist attack to be livestreamed across social media to a global audience, but it was the first to go viral.

All terrorist attacks are to some degree performative, but the twenty-eight-year-old gunman went to extraordinary lengths to appeal to and engage an online global audience to spread his message of hatred and violence. Minutes before the Facebook livestream commenced, copies of his self-penned manifesto were linked to posts he made on social media platforms Twitter and 8chan. A URL to the livestream and words of encouragement to online followers were included so that others would access, share, and spread the attack in real time. The helmet camera resulted in nearly seventeen minutes of high-definition, point-of-view violence that purposefully replicated a first-person video game. A "backing track" made up of anti-Islamic songs, popular among the denizens of online far-right chat forums such as 4chan and 8chan, was played through a speaker strapped to a weapon. This was interspersed with instructional commentary as the attacker discussed the effectiveness of his weapons and attempted to glorify his violence through direct appeals to the audience. The weapons themselves were graffitied with symbols and phrases, such as "kebab killer," referring to popular online racist memes. Perhaps most revealingly, just before the attack the terrorist made a direct comment to the camera saying, "Remember lads, subscribe to PewDiePie," referencing Swedish YouTuber Fellix Kjellberg. Kjellberg, who had been accused of using far-right material in his clips, was at the time the world's top-subscribed YouTuber and in a race with Bollywood music channel T-Series to be the first to reach 100 million subscribers (Dickson 2019).

As the attack took place, only a limited number of online followers encouraged and cheered on the attacker in real time (Lowe 2019). However, copies of the footage soon began to spread across digital media. In the first twenty-four hours after the attack, Facebook moderators removed 1.5 million uploads. At over two billion users, Facebook represents by far the biggest audience in history. During the same period, YouTube removed tens of thousands of versions of the clip (it has not released exact numbers), many of them altered by users in an attempt to evade automated censor software. At one point, the number of new clips of the attack being uploaded to YouTube reached one per second, while hundreds of new accounts were created solely to share versions of the livestream. Some mainstream media also posted clips of the attack online, with six minutes of raw video footage being posted by Australian news.com.au showing the gunman driving on his way to the attack (Murrell 2019). Days after the attack, Facebook's former chief information security officer Alex Stamos posted on Twitter that searches surged as "millions of people are being told online and on TV that there is a video and a document that are too dangerous for them to see" (Bogle 2019).

In the wake of the Christchurch attack, governments and social media companies scrambled to address the danger that terrorism and violent extremism on the Internet supposedly pose to vulnerable audiences online. Internet service providers in New Zealand blocked access to lesser-regulated platforms such as 4chan, 8chan, and LiveLeak (Ilascu 2019), while Reddit banned the subreddits WatchPeopleDie and Gore due to their glorifying of the attacks. Australia introduced legislation fining platforms and potentially imprisoning their executives if they did not remove terrorist content; its Prime Minister stated that social media companies must "take every possible action to ensure their technology products are not exploited by murderous terrorists" (Fingas 2019). On the international stage, New Zealand and France led the Christchurch Call, a global effort to hold social media companies to account for promoting terrorism by eliminating terrorist and violent extremist content online. This was because "such content online has adverse impacts on the human rights of the victims, on our collective security and on people all over the world" (Christchurch Call n.d.). The New Zealand Classification Office (n.d.), in banning the livestream, was blunt about the dangers it believed were posed by online violent extremist material, stating that those "who are susceptible to radicalisation may well be encouraged or emboldened."

One year after the Christchurch attack, we, as academics at Macquarie University in New South Wales, the Australian state from which the attacker hailed, conducted focus groups with young people about their emotions and experiences when accessing terrorism and violent extremism online. Almost without exception these young people had accessed the Christchurch attack, either the full livestream or partial clips. What we saw was surprising. Instead of evidence for radicalisation, the young people we talked to revealed complex emotional responses and behaviours. For one participant, the attack was an affront to their online culture. They were shocked that their humour had been appropriated by a terrorist, but this did not result in them abandoning their online culture:

> Yeah, that [references the Christchurch attack] – and it ruined the humour behind the subscribe to PewDiePie. After that moment, I was just – or that humour about his subscribe to PewDiePie, let's take over the world. Then I – it just – those jokes just weren't really funny at all. I remember seeing that and that just completely really broke something for me and I was just like oh, this guy is gross. This guy has the same sort of humour as me. He has a similar culture, meme culture and stuff – humour, as me and he's doing all those terrible things that moved me away from that meme culture, I guess. But obviously, I'm still into it, so, yeah, I was like woah.

This Element is about young people, online terrorism, and emotion. In it, we explore the issues of how young people consume violent extremist material in the digital era: how it makes them feel, what they do with this content and these feelings afterwards, and how they talk about it with friends and family. If the Christchurch attack was "engineered for maximum virality" (Warzel 2019), a design principle that has since been emulated by far-right extremists in El Paso (Zekulin 2019) and Singapore (Walden 2021), then this Element is about the generation who have been targeted as the online audience. Yet despite almost universal concern from a number of quarters, including parents, the media, government, and tech companies, there have been surprisingly few attempts to initiate conversations with young people themselves about their emotions and the effects on them of exposure to online terrorism and violent extremism. This is surprising given that so few of these young people actually become terrorists. There is a lot of concern in this space, but not a lot of conversation.

Emotions, Terrorism and the Audience

The incorporation of the word "terror" in terrorism, defined here as "the state of being terrified or extremely frightened; an instance or feeling of this" (Oxford English Dictionary, n.d.), creates an inescapable relationship between the phenomenon of terrorism and emotion. Yet any study of emotions within the discipline of terrorism studies has been largely absent. In part this reflects a perspective of emotions as unconscious and beyond the control of an individual, and therefore problematising the presentation of terrorism as the product of rational decision-making (Crawford 2000, 124). Notable exceptions include studies by Neta Crawford and by David Wright-Neville and Debra Smith (Crawford 2000; Wright-Neville and Smith 2009). The distinction between positive and negative emotions has been shown by scholars within the history of emotions to be a function of history, with simple dichotomies restricting more complex analysis (Solomon 2008). However, the binary demarcation of positive and negative emotions remains in use among scholars examining emotions in the context of violent extremism. This is reflected in the tendency of terrorism scholarship to focus on negative emotions both among victims (terror, hurt, fear) and among perpetrators (humiliation, anger, hate). The focus on these types of emotions, as will be discussed here, is certainly valid. However there remains the possibility that other emotions arise, including positive emotions such as love, happiness, relief, and compassion (Cottee and Hayward 2011, 975). Examining the intersection between emotion, social structures, political processes, and individual perceptions and/or behaviours can provide insights into the complex dynamics involved in processes of radicalisation to violent extremism (Wright-Neville and Smith 2009).

Although writing prior to the global dissemination of digital media, Neta Crawford's comments remain acutely relevant:

> Just as emotions are labile, emotional relationships may be altered. So, the categorization of a group's emotional relationship to another group, and therefore the behaviours a group deems normatively obliged to enact, may change if empathy or antipathy are elicited through contact (Crawford 2000, 135).

Her statement reflects the critical requirement for systematic examination of the relationships between emotions, violent extremism, and digital media to understand how, why, and when online content may (or may not) contribute to processes of radicalisation to violence. By marginalising the role emotions play in violent extremism, we risk returning to a one-dimensional model of radicalisation that pitches the all-powerful violent extremist against the vulnerable and passive individual.

Examining the spectrum of emotions also provides insight into the emergence of the moral panic that has arisen in response to the presence of violent extremist content on digital media and the framing of youth audiences as particularly vulnerable. It helps to problematise the notion that "technical things have political qualities ... and the claim that the machines ... can embody specific forms of power and authority" (Winner 1996; Nahon 2015, 19). Prioritising emotions in this way demands a reconceptualisation of the complexity of this "vulnerable" audience while identifying opportunities to strengthen and develop resilience to violent extremism at an individual, group, and societal level.

Understanding the audience is key to any appreciation of how or why terrorists engage in violence the way that they do, and why, since the advent of digital media, terrorists themselves have been so dedicated to posting violence online. According to most definitions, terrorism can usefully be thought of as an audience-focused performance of violence. The violent act is intended to create strong negative emotions (i.e., terror and fear) among those who are impacted by the violence, or who hear about it or view it through media reporting. Strategically, terrorism is a remarkably successful form of political violence due to this ability to cultivate widespread fear among an audience, particularly when this popular fear is then translated into demands for political elites to respond to the provocation in some way (Freedman 1983). Responses can include accommodating the terrorist's demands, that is, for political concessions such as the autonomy or emancipation of a group, or forms of unintended state overreaction that put further pressure on the society that is under attack (Altheide 2006). In this way, it is no exaggeration to say that terrorism is in essence a strategy of political violence that relies on the manipulation of negative emotions, particularly anxiety, fear, and terror, among an audience usually made up of the general public.

It is surprising therefore that, given the central role audience emotion plays in the success of terrorist strategy, there has been relatively little attention placed by terrorism researchers on the range of emotional responses felt by audiences who view media reporting of terrorist acts. As we will see, those studies that have been conducted have mostly been in relation to traditional media, particularly newspapers and television, and not the new media landscape characterised by the Internet, digital platforms, and social media (Aly 2017). The majority of academic considerations of the audiences of terrorist attacks have focused their analysis on various classifications of the audiences into types. These include the uncommitted versus the sympathetic (Wright 1991), immediate victims versus neutral groups (Schmid 2005), or government versus media (Matusitz 2012). Although useful for thinking about how terrorists perform their violence and frame their media so as to impact various groups, this research does not reveal the variety of emotional responses, perceptions, and responses held by audiences themselves to the terrorist content they consume.

What we do know is that emotions such as fear, anxiety, and even trauma are not uncommon audience reactions to terrorist violence, even when that exposure is purely through media reporting (Sinclair and Antonius 2012; Kiper and Sosis 2015). For years after the September 11, 2001, attacks by al-Qaeda, for example, polls showed terrorism remained the highest-ranking fear among American youth (Lyons 2005). Research on human subjects has demonstrated that media exposure to terrorist events can create audience fear and sympathy (Iyer and Oldmeadow 2006), depression, and anxiety (Norris, Kern, and Just 2003), as well as lingering posttraumatic stress (in this case among children) (Pfefferbaum et al. 2003). This is despite the fact that the high levels of fear engendered by terrorism are usually disproportionate to the actual risks terrorism poses in Western countries, certainly when compared with other less sensationalised dangers such as homicides, domestic violence, or traffic accidents (Matusitz 2012).

Indeed, research on audiences who have been exposed to terrorist violence through traditional media show that media saturation following a terrorist attack can result in "mean world" syndrome whereby audiences overestimate the risk of becoming the victim of terrorism and demonstrate an irrational desire for overprotection (Matusitz 2012). This overreaction to negative emotions has been shown to manifest as a form of catastrophising in which audience members feel either increased aggression towards out-groups, particularly when they share the same religion or ethnicity as the terrorists (Kiper and Sosis 2015), or an opposite fear that encourages capitulation to terrorist demands (Iyer et al. 2015). This ability of media exposure to terrorism to create fear, anxiety, anger, aggression, and prejudice towards an out-group has been shown to be more pronounced than in media about other forms of crime (Shoshani and Slone 2008; Nellis and Savage 2012).

The type of media through which terrorism is experienced also plays a role in how audiences respond. Sensationalised and tabloid news coverage has been shown, for example, to lead to the adoption of more negative emotions and hawkish foreign policy positions among American subjects (Gadarian 2010). These effects have also found to increase when exposure is through a visual medium such as television, and especially when graphic and evocative imagery is used (Gadarian 2014). Vergani (2018) found that terrorism is perceived as more threatening by audiences living in countries dominated by market-oriented commercial and tabloid media. He suggests this is due to commercial media's focus on entertainment and on arousing the emotions and passions of viewers, in part through sensationalising terrorist events. This contrasts with public-oriented media that emphasises factual non-emotive reporting, which correspondingly results in an audience that feel less terrified and threatened by anxieties about terrorism.

The research that we refer to above has tended to focus on traditional, rather than digital, media. It assumes viewers that are relatively passive and view news through traditional mediums such as print and broadcast media. However, in the digital environment there is a fundamental shift in the nature of audience responses and in how people expect to and do interact with media on different platforms and in differing contexts. Using these platforms, it is well-established that audiences become both consumers and producers of content. They are, in other words, part of the process of interacting with and disseminating content (variously termed "prosumers" or "produsers"), as a form of entertainment and social engagement (Ritzer and Jurgenson 2010; Bruns 2007). Indeed, research on how audiences receive terrorism content online, on how it makes them feel and act, is conspicuously missing (Aly 2017). Hence, most commentary about how online audiences experience terrorist content, or even become radicalised to violence, only speculates on the nature and extent of their impressions and how they are influenced. As noted by Aly (2017) this sort of commentary is "often based on an assumption that the violent extremist narrative works like a magic bullet to radicalise audiences already vulnerable and predisposed to becoming violent."

In part, this assumption about the dangers of exposure to online terrorist content and the vulnerability of audiences reflects the application of a media-effects theory framework in understanding how exposure to digital media may lead to radicalisation to violence. A foundational theorist of the media-effects school of thought was Albert Bandura, a Canadian-American psychologist who used social science experiments to demonstrate that, by observing behaviours, people – and particularly children – learn to model behaviours and emotions. This model was then cross-applied to the theory that, by watching and absorbing media of various forms, vulnerable groups would be stimulated to mimic the behaviour and would be effectively desensitized. The best-known critic of this framework for understanding how people, and particularly young people, respond to media stimuli, including violent video games, is David Gauntlett, a British sociologist and media studies theorist. In his influential essay, *Ten Things Wrong with the Media "Effects" Model*, he argues that reputable crim-inologists consistently rank media engagement as one of the least influential factors among the causes of real-world violence (Gauntlett 1998). He notes that media effects studies are consistently conducted in artificial laboratory type settings which ignore the multiple factors that influence how and why media consumers view material and the role that their pre-existing values and cultural and socio-economic backgrounds and experiences play in those interactions. Indeed, in their systematic review of protective and risk factors for radicalisa-tion, Wolfowicz et al. (2020) noted the limited effect of direct and passive exposure to violent media in generating risks associated with radicalisation (Wolfowicz et al. 2020).

Overall, despite the shocking nature of terrorist violence going viral online, and the very clear strategy used by groups and individuals such as the so-called Islamic State and the Christchurch attacker in hijacking the Internet and social media to spread their propaganda, we still know very little about how this material affects young people. Assumptions taken from the field of terrorism research and traditional media-effects theory suggest that the primary emotional response to this material must be terror, or something like it, and that the result must be trauma or even radicalisation to violence. However, we do not know if these assumptions are valid, particularly in the context of the blended online environments through which young people increasingly inhabit and mediate their social relationships. This Element, and the research that informs it, explore this new environment through the voices and experiences of young people themselves.

The Research Project

The genesis of this research came about in early 2015. That year saw a rapid rise in concern among the government, the media, and the general public about the dangers the Internet posed to young people who were being increasingly exposed to violent extremism online, particularly through digital media. The succeeding twenty-four months became something of a watershed for fears about the confluence of terrorism, the Internet, and "vulnerable" youth. The so-called Islamic State (IS) had commenced a global online media campaign that was tech-savvy, aimed at youth, and beginning to result in large numbers of people – often young people – leaving their homes to join IS's self-styled caliphate (Bergin et al. 2015). Others, once connected to the extensive and well-funded online IS networks, were remaining home and supporting the group in other ways: as financiers, recruiters, propagandists, or even as violent actors. Around this core of terrorists and their supporters a larger, grayer area was coalescing; this was made up of IS "fanboys" and "fangirls" using the Internet and social media to create and spread violent and extreme pro-Islamic State memes, songs and video games (Winter 2015). At the same time, schools began to report an emergent phenomenon of "Jihadi cool" among students, a transgressive subculture adopted by rebellious youth, sometimes as young as primary school age (Cottee 2015). It is not surprising that increasingly frantic questions began to be asked by concerned parents, teachers, politicians, and national security practitioners about the vulnerability of youth on the Internet. Was a whole generation being radicalised overnight via their mobile phones and social media accounts? In this climate of uncertainty and fear, there was no shortage of terrorism commentators and instant experts warning that online violent extremism presented a new and sinister threat that adults and established security agencies were completely unequipped to counter (Burke 2015).

As academic researchers working in the fields of terrorism studies and media studies, we began to ask questions about this phenomenon. Just what is the role of the Internet in creating terrorists? In particular, how exactly was online violent extremist content received, interpreted, and processed by young people them-selves? Why, given the volume and frequency of engagement with this type of content, were so many young people *not* becoming radicalised to violent extremism? It was clear that there were major gaps in our understanding of terrorism and the Internet regarding the role and influence of online violent extremist messaging on the phenomenon of radicalisation. While literature in the field acknowledged that the Internet played some part in radicalisation processes for some people and in some circumstances, there was little actual evidence to support assumptions of causality between young people accessing online violent extremist content and becoming radicalised to violent extremism (Von Behr et al. 2013).

As concern about online youth radicalisation grew, and as Islamic State's propaganda was joined – and then superseded – by online far-right violence and extremism, one thing became increasingly apparent: for all the attention given by the media and government to this problem nobody was asking young people (Frissen 2021). Their experiences navigating these difficult online spaces, and their own ideas about what constituted "violent" and "extreme" content, were not being recorded or considered. Nor were their emotional responses and strategies of coping. Here we present our research with young people reflecting and talking about how they navigate violent extremist material online, how it makes them feel, what they do with these emotions afterwards, how they talk about them with friends and adults, and their experiences of the contested process of radicalisation. Through this, we hope to reinsert the voices and experiences of young people into a debate that has not gone away but that has only intensified over the succeeding years.

The young people who generously gave us their time and trust to discuss their experiences, during what became an increasingly anxious time as Covid-19 made its mark on Australian campuses, are referred to as "participants" throughout. Quotations from participants are in general verbatim, although some minor modifications were made at times and when necessary for purposes of anonymity. Numeric references are used to indicate a discussion between different participants within a single focus group, while all other quotes reflect comments from a single participant.

Definitions

The arguments presented below rely on two key terms – "violent extremism" and "digital media." Our definitions for these complex and contested phenomena are set out here.

Violent Extremism

There is little consensus in the literature as to the definition of violent extremism. Its popularity in academic and policy circles arose in part to address the intrinsic relationship between terrorism and the politics of power. The term has found itself intertwined with political narratives of power, exclusion, and control, and as such is drowning in definitional complexity (Elzain 2008, 10). We use the definition of extremism by J. M. Berger who in turn draws on social psychological theories of social identity (Berger 2018). Reflecting the findings of the work presented here, this definition is centred on the primacy of social relationships and the tendency of these to generate distinctions between in-groups and out-groups based on perceived social connections. These differences are not necessarily problematic and, as Berger notes, are often celebrated within pluralistic societies. Violent extremism occurs when an out-group is systematically demonised and positioned as an acute crisis for the survival of the in-group, necessitating decisive and hostile action against the out-group (Berger 2018, 121–122).

The work of Manus Midlarsky (2011) provides a theoretical model for why an out-group may be framed as a threat to the survival of an in-group, and how this can lead to the creation of extremist social movements willing to perpetrate violence and murder. Midlarsky argues that a loss of political and social authority by an in-group can lead to deeply felt perceptions of injustice and mass emotions of anger, shame, and humiliation. This shared perception by the in-group opens a cognitive window allowing dehumanisation, violence, and even the extermination of those considered to be the problem. Although Midlarsky's framework relies on a consideration of the shared emotions of masses, rather than the emotions of individuals and their contribution to collective social movements, it remains useful in keeping us alert to the foundational emotional drivers of violent extremism and terrorism.

Online violent extremist content may be expressed in multiple ways, drawing on humour, satire, glorification, and deniability to attract and speak to different audiences. However, underpinning all these variations is a commitment to a polarised way of viewing the world that is intolerant to dissent. It is a view of the world whereby the survival of the in-group requires the destruction of the out-group.

Digital Media

In the focus groups we conducted, the environment under examination was usually referred to as "social media" with the unspoken assumption this covered social media platforms such as Facebook, Instagram, and TikTok as well as tools such as Google and Wikipedia. However, it became increasingly clear that participants engaged with traditional legacy media sources such as newspapers and television through online mediums. These mediums in turn were far more than just channels for transferring information but represented what Simon Lindgren describes as *"environments* for social interaction" (Lindgren 2017, 4). This complexity has led to a shift in the discipline towards the adoption of the term "digital media" to capture the blurring of both traditional and new media with online and offline environments. While this term usefully captures the combination of co-existing forms of information and technologies, we remain cognisant of the risk that removing "social" from the phrase will muffle the fundamentally important relationship between human emotion, behaviour, and technology. While technology is by no means a passive phenomenon, it is essentially humans that make and use technology. Digital media should therefore be read as an enabling environment, within which interactions occur, that facilitates dynamic social relationships between people, information, and technology.

2 Youth and Online Violent Extremism

The surveys and discussions with young people about their experiences of terrorism and violent extremism online that are presented here come from research conducted between 2015 and 2020. This research project, supported by an Australian Research Council Discovery Project grant, focused on examining how youth audiences interact with online violent extremist content, during and after exposure. Considering that terrorists undertake attacks and spread propaganda primarily to instil the emotion of terror in an intended audience, and to then leverage this terror to their own advantage, we were particularly interested in finding out more about the feelings, perceptions, and emotions that young people experienced when interacting with online violent extremism. Through recording how online violent extremist messages are received, interpreted, discussed, and reflected upon by youth audiences, we hoped to develop a baseline of evidence about the strategies of resistance and resilience employed by those inhabiting these online spaces. Both research and experience attest that the overwhelming majority of people, of whatever age, who experience violent and extreme content online do not become radicalised to violent extremism, let alone join terrorist organisations (Conway 2017). This being the case, the interaction between young people and online violent extremist content, particularly the emotions they feel when exposed, must be more complex, nuanced, and subtle than dominant discourses suggest.

Our research involved a mixed-method investigation into young people's experiences online, divided into two main phases. The first phase was broadly quantitative and exploratory. It drew on the results of online quantitative polling of approximately 1,000 Australian young people between twelve and twenty-four years of age, and asked about aspects of their experiences with online violent extremism. As will be discussed below, this survey data was part of a broader online polling commissioned by the Advocate for Children and Young People (ACYP), who used a certified social market research company to conduct the research in line with industry standards and regulations. The second phase was broadly qualitative, building a set of more in-depth questions based on the findings from the earlier survey. It consisted of a series of seven in-depth focus group discussions with young people between the ages of eighteen and twenty-four. These focus groups were structured around open and semi-structured discussions among young people and facilitated by the three-person research team. The focus groups and use of the survey data were conducted in compliance with Macquarie University Human Research Ethics (No: 52019347312409). This required that all participants sign a consent form that detailed the difficult nature of the subject matter, specified that we would not be providing new or explicit content during the focus groups, and explained how information and activities of interest to legal authorities were not to be discussed. To mitigate the possibility of distress to participants, we provided the details of relevant support services including those of the helpline StepTogether that specialises in countering violent extremism and of broader counselling providers. The information was reiterated at the beginning and end of each focus group.

Both the survey and the focus groups were carried out in the Australian state of New South Wales (NSW) between mid-2018 and the beginning of 2020. The two phases were designed to capture the experiences and voices of the generation in which social media and smartphone use has become almost ubiquitous. Many of the young people we surveyed and talked with had experienced the rapid expansion of Islamic State and far-right violence and extremism online, had been part of friendship circles in which online violent extremism and terrorism were discussed and had become key social touchstones, and had seemingly found ways to navigate these difficult spaces successfully. It should be noted that the young people we surveyed were also part of a generation that had been impacted by heightened parental, school, and government concern about the dangers of terrorism on the Internet and the possibilities of youth radicalisation (Bergin et al. 2015).

This mixed-method design incorporating both quantitative and qualitative data was employed in order to build empirically on what is known about young people's experiences of online violent extremism, rather than on what commentators assume (or fear) about it. In addition, rather than repeating the numerous studies attempting research into the elusive process of online radicalisation (Meleagrou-Hitchens, Alexander, and Kaderbhai 2017), we decided to explore the wider issue of how young people interact, both emotionally and behaviourally, with online violent extremism. Instead of looking for the "one in ten thousand" who become radicalised to terrorism, we were more interested in how the full cohort and their friends navigated this space, the problems they faced, and the solutions they devised. It is our contention that it is impossible to understand radicalisation to violence online, and the risks that it poses to youth, without first gaining a clearer picture of the diverse ways young people have themselves devised to engage emotionally and behaviourally with these difficult online spaces.

Phase One: The Survey

The survey was carried out in collaboration with the NSW Office of the Advocate for Children and Young People (ACYP). The Advocate has existed since 2014 as an independent statutory office reporting to the New South Wales Parliament in Australia. Its aim is to advocate for the well-being of children and young people through promoting youth agency in decisions that affect their lives, to make recommendations on policy, and to conduct research into issues that affect children and young people. We partnered with the Advocate because of our shared concern for young people and interest in better understanding the context within which online violent extremism is accessed, experienced, and reacted to.

We included five questions related to young people's experiences of online violent extremism in a broader attitudinal survey the Advocate commissioned in June 2018. The survey was distributed online to a representative sample of young people between the ages of twelve and twenty-four from across New South Wales, attracting approximately 1,005 respondents. All questions were presented through with simple multiple choice or drop-down-style answers. The questions were:

1. Have you experienced extremism online?
2. Where was the place that this online extremism was experienced?
3. What is the reason why you considered the experience to be extreme?
4. How did the experience of extreme content make you feel?
5. What action did you take after experiencing this extreme content?

One limitation of this phase of the research was our inability to ask specifically about "violent" extremism online. The reluctance to question young people about experiences of violence through a large government-sponsored online survey stemmed from duty of care responsibilities should any responses indicate engagement with violent extremism or terrorist activities. The absence of references to violence from the questions, however, did not prevent young people from reflecting on and reporting violent extremism in their answers. This is because experiences of specifically violent extremist content would presumably still be considered to have been "extreme," and hence reported and recorded in the survey.

Phase Two: The Focus Groups

The focus groups were carried out in partnership with Macquarie University, located in Sydney, Australia. Seven focus group sessions were held in early 2020 on the university campus. These were ended suddenly in early 2020 due to the interruption caused by the Covid-19 pandemic and by the abrupt cessation of all face-to-face research due to university and government social distancing policies. Each focus group lasted for one hour, and consisted of members of the research team and a group of young people aged between eighteen and twenty-four years. Participants were drawn from the under-graduate cohort at Macquarie University; approximately half were domestic Australian and half were international students, mostly from the Asia Pacific. There was an attempt to balance between genders in recruiting focus group participants. The focus groups were advertised through campus-wide paper flyers and direct emails to student cohorts within the Faculty of Arts. Advertisements specifically asked for volunteers who had experienced violent or extreme material online and who were willing to talk about these experi-ences in a safe and non-judgmental environment. Participants were reim-bursed with a $20 (AU) coffee voucher. Focus groups were purposely kept small and intimate to allow an in-depth and qualitatively rich discussion about their experiences. Each session had a minimum of three and a maximum of seven participants. In total, twenty-five young people partici-pated in the discussions; each had previously reported having had significant experiences of online violent extremism.

Focus group sessions were recorded and later transcribed by an outside company. These transcripts were then analysed by the project team through NVivo software using a grounded theory approach. Any identifying character-istics of participants, such as name, age, nationality, and so on were removed through the transcription process. In this way, participants were anonymised in a way that ensured their privacy and safety, and that encouraged open and frank discussion about their online experiences. Participants were notified that while the research team were not collecting information about any illegal behaviour, any disclosures of such activity would be reported to authorities in line with legislative requirements.

Focus group discussions were kept open-ended to allow the young people to raise and reflect on the issues that have affected them, rather than on those that terrorism experts assume to be most important. At the same time, each focus group was structured around the same series of key questions and themes posed by the research team. These questions were designed to explore how young people defined violent extremism, how it made them feel emotionally, what they subsequently did with the material, why they thought this material was produced, and whether they discussed these experiences with friends or adults. The research team made a conscious decision to neither define violent extremism at the outset, nor to mention the terms "terrorism," "terrorist," "radicalisation," or notable types of terrorism such as "al-Qaeda," "Islamic State," or "the far right." This was done in order to not seed the participants with expectations about the types of violent extremism that researchers might be most interested in, familiar with, or consider to be of most concern. Nor did we want young people to be prompted into thinking we were most concerned with issues or mechanisms of radicalisation to terrorism. Instead, young people told us what most concerned them online, what they found to be violent and extreme, and how it made them feel and act. Even with these conscious absences, incidents of terrorism (particularly Islamic State and the far-right Christchurch massacre livestream) were raised during each focus group and were animatedly discussed by all the participants. Participants recalled incidents of terrorism and violent extremism online but had minimal knowledge of the specifics of group names, movements, and political contexts. Our strategy of initiating a truly open discussion about violent extremism online resulted in a wider and more diverse understanding than is usually found in the terrorism literature about the nature of this difficult environment and how it is navigated by youth.

Young People and Online Extremism

The following section details the results of the 2018 survey of the general youth population about their experiences online. It presents results pertaining to fundamental questions that remain unanswered or debated in this space. These are: whether young people experience extremism online; where they experience it; how they define "extreme"; how it made them feel emotionally; and what they did with this content afterward. These questions provide the foundational context for a more detailed discussion in later sections about the emotional experiences and subsequent behaviours of young people.

The questions about where this material was accessed online and, most importantly, about what they consider to be violent and extreme are supplemented by research taken from the in-depth focus groups. This was done to give the reader a fuller comprehension of the nature of these foundational issues and questions before moving on to the focus group discussions in Sections 3, 4, and 5.

Have You Experienced Extremism Online?

The survey revealed that, as shown in Figure 1, just over one in ten (12 per cent) of young people reported experiencing extremism online. A much larger number, two-thirds (67 per cent), said that they have not, and 22 per cent didn't know. The large percentage who marked "don't know" could reflect confusion about the meaning of "extremism," a term that is not necessarily self-evident despite high levels of public and media debate and concern over recent years. A similar finding was noted in the 2018 Australian survey by the e-safety commissioner (State of Play 2018) where only 25 per cent of young people reported "negative experiences online," indicating that extremism makes up only one aspect of the perceived negative aspects of youths' online experiences. Emerging research from beyond Australia suggests that these figures should not be taken as representing universal experiences.

The numbers represented in Figure 1 contain a significant level of diversity. Older respondents (nineteen to twenty-four years old) were slightly more likely than younger ones (twelve to eighteen years old) to have experienced extremism, as were those who did not speak English at home. Males were more likely, at 14 per cent, to have experienced extremism online than females (9 per cent), mirroring research that consistently shows that while violent extremist material affects both males and females, it affects males at a higher

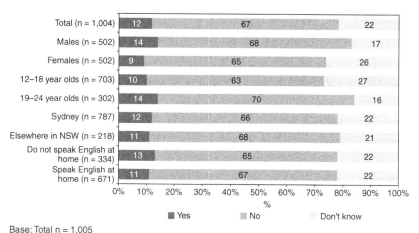

Base: Total n = 1,005
QB44: Have you ever experienced extremism online?

Figure 1 Have you ever experienced extremism online?

rate (Möller-Leimkühler 2018). Those with a disability were much more likely, at 26 per cent, to have reported experiencing extremism online. One way of explaining this disparity is that it may reflect an increased amount of time spent online by those who identify as disabled, or alternatively it may reflect higher levels of discrimination faced. This may be particularly significant in light of the subsequent Covid-19 pandemic and elevated time spent online generally.

Where Did You Experience Extremism Online?

The places online where children and young people reported that they had experienced extreme content were, in descending order, Facebook (34 per cent), Instagram (16 per cent), and YouTube (16 per cent), followed by "social media generally" (15 per cent) (Figure 2). This broadly reflects the popularity of the main social media platforms among youth at this time, and prior to the growth of later popular sites such as TikTok or Parler. The absence of peer-to-peer encrypted sites such as Telegram or WhatsApp, as well as niche sites such as Gab, is notable. However, it is possible that some experiences on these platforms may have been captured in the large percentage (10 per cent) listed as "other."

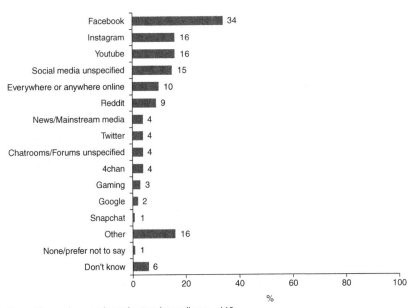

Base: Those who experienced extremism online n = 110
QB46: Where online have you experienced extreme content?

Figure 2 Where online have you experienced extreme content?

Alarmingly, a full 10 per cent of respondents claimed that extremism was "everywhere and anywhere" online, while 4 per cent saw it in the news and mainstream media. These figures reinforce an understanding of the blurred distinction between social media and legacy mass media, and even between the offline and online domains. The inclusion of mass media does suggest that isolating and elevating social media as an exceptional or separate realm does not adequately reflect the realities of young people's experiences. This is backed by responses from the later focus groups held in 2020 and reiterates the need to conceptualise digital media as a spectrum of media types old, new, online, offline, and other.

There was a persistent willingness during the focus groups for participants to list non-social media platforms as notable online spaces where they have come across violent or extreme content. Netflix was mentioned a number of times, in particular the US documentary *Don't F**k with Cats: Hunting an Internet Killer*, which follows the online manhunt for an animal abuser who later murdered an international student. *The Trials of Gabriel Fernandez*, a US true crime serial depicting the abuse and murder of an eight-year-old boy was also noted, as was the 2019 film *Joker*. Although produced for popular consumption and accessed through online streaming platforms, these TV shows, documentaries, and films were talked about in a way that showed that they had shocked some viewers. These fictionalised or documentary depictions of violent extremism also provided frames of reference through which the depictions of real-world online violent extremism were later interpreted and understood. According to one participant:

> I got Facebook when I was quite older, so when I was 17, 18, so I didn't really have that much access to all these online platforms at a young age. I would say the most violent extremism that I can remember was actually through TV. There was a documentary about a shooting in a high school in America. I remember all the details. I remember thinking that can happen, this happens. Every time a shooting does happen, I always think back to that and think back to – because they showed footage from what the kids had and screaming and fear and all. So every time something like that comes up, I always think back to when I watched that.

A smaller number of participants described news videos from mainstream media sites depicting organised crime or state violence by the police or armed forces as online violent extremism. These were discussed in relation to the Philippines and Chile specifically, and the clips were generally seen on Facebook. Surprisingly, no participants described online gaming platforms as the location where they experienced violent or extreme content.

In terms of the digital media platforms discussed, participants reported accessing violent extremist materials on a range of sites that closely align with the broader survey data described above, and that mirror the relative popularity of sites used by young people at the time. Facebook was by far the most discussed platform, making up more than half of all references in our sample. This is notable as it contradicts the popular assertions and some research (Anderson and Jiang 2018) that suggests Facebook has lost currency among young people, and that they are departing the platform for more niche sites. Our experience suggests that Facebook has been the primary platform through which young people experience violent and extreme material, at least in recent years. Following Facebook, the relative popularity of platforms mentioned during the focus groups were: Instagram and YouTube in equal second place, and then Twitter and Reddit in equal third, followed by Snapchat. Lesser visited sites that were mentioned fewer than five times included 4chan, WhatsApp, and Tumblr. Sites that have recently been associated with far-right extremism and violent content, such as 8chan/8kun and Gab, were not mentioned at all.

One site that was mentioned on three separate occasions was LiveLeak. This is an extreme and voyeuristic file-sharing and streaming service designed to make available extreme, taboo, and violent material. As expected, although this site was only mentioned on a handful of occasions, it was associated with ultra-violent material such as Islamic State beheading videos and footage of the Christchurch attack. According to one participant:

> They have all these uncensored, really violent videos and I'd watch the ISIS execution videos. I'd watch it for fun, but I felt like that desensitized me towards a lot of things. I somehow managed to get hold of the Christchurch shooting footage as well last year. I think that was the first time in my life where I actually got a bit concerned about it, about my health.

What Do You Consider to be Violent or Extreme?

One of the most contentious questions facing digital media platforms, users, and governments is also seemingly the simplest – what exactly is violent extremist content? This was one of the first questions asked during the 2018 survey, the results of which can be seen in Figure 3. It is perhaps unsurprising that 17 per cent of respondents classified religious extremism, ISIS, jihad, terrorism, and/or beheading as violent extremist content. This type of terrorist content, including the livestream footage of the Christchurch attack, was also frequently referenced by the focus group participants:

> There was a video where it was all young – twelve–thirteen – teenagers, and they were all just kneeling down and then they were saying something in their

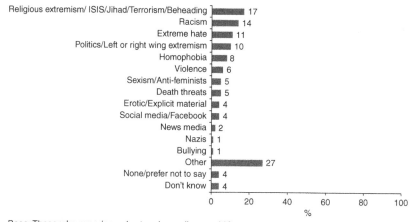

Base: Those who experienced extremism online n = 110
QB45: Can you describe why you considered what you experienced to be extreme?

Figure 3 Can you describe why you considered what you experienced to be extreme?

language. With guns and I think they started shooting . . . that's the first thing that I think of.

Results of both the survey and focus group highlight the complexity underpinning classifications of what should be labelled online violent extremism. As demonstrated in Figure 3, survey respondents categorised homophobic, sexism or anti-feminist, and death threats as representative of extreme content. Interestingly, the highest frequency category selected by survey participants was "other" (27 per cent). The use of this catch-all term may indicate a lack of understanding among respondents as to the meaning of the question. This uncertainty was also reflected in the focus groups. For example, it was not uncommon for participants to discuss whether something counted as violent extremism, saying things like: "I don't know – does it count? – someone on my Facebook went through a phase of posting pictures of foetuses."

It is also possible that for some respondents the pre-given survey categories (based on usual interpretations of violent extremist content found in the terrorism studies literature and in media reporting) did not accurately capture their perceptions of extreme online content. This breadth in definitions for violent extreme content is increasingly paralleled in mainstream discussions of the blurred line between hate speech, incitement of violence, and expressions of negative emotions such as disgust, anger, dislike, and so on. Indeed, it has increasingly become "inherently difficult to define objective parameters for something as value-laden as highly political ideological discourse," of which violent extremism is perhaps the greatest example (Holbrook 2015, 64).

This diversity of content labelled as "violent extremism" was reiterated in the focus groups. Again, Netflix documentaries such as *Don't F**K with Cats: Hunting an Internet Killer, The Trials of Gabriel Fernandez* and *Surviving R. Kelly* were all raised and discussed by participants as examples of online violent extremism. The inclusion of these types of content highlights the melding of traditional and new forms of media (Pascoe 2011). Participants' discussions around these documentaries, as well as real-world events such as the Columbine school shooting, point to the challenges that arise from the inherent dynamism associated with online content production. While the initial event or film was classified by young people as violent extremism, they also discussed the emergence of linked memes, music videos, and commentary that they classified as humorous. For example, memes of R. Kelly and the song *Pumped Up Kicks* made about the Columbine shooting were discussed more in terms of humour and/or celebrity status. As one participant noted with respect to the transformation of violent extremist content: "You just kind of make fun of what we think – like what's usually evil or what's usually violent, as a joke."

The diversity of violence captured in the focus group discussions also reflected the presence of voyeuristic platforms that host video content depicting a range of violent acts such as people dying or being involved in car crashes. Here participants were unclear as to the intentionality of the act noting how it "could be purposeful or it could be accidental." This is an interesting observation particularly given the importance granted to the attribution of purpose within traditional definitions of violent extremism. This diversity of violence is also reflected in the inclusion of gang-related violence as falling within violent extremist classifications. Participants described their experiences of viewing violence perpetrated by Mexican cartels and Brazilian gang-related shootings. Sexual violence was also cited by participants as an example of violent extremist content. Participants described encountering videos that depicted acts of graphic violence against women; for example, one user described a video where "it's a dead body of a woman, and her – this part is cut open and someone … this guy was penetrating her. It was really graphic." They also classified mainstream media reporting of sexual assaults against women in conflict zones, such as the stoning of Yazidi women, as examples of violent extremist content.

One of the atypical categories that emerged from the focus groups was animal-rights content. Discussions often pointed to the presence of videos and images that documented the abuse of animals, including slaughter and torture. There was a degree of nuance in the applicability of the term "violent extremism" for some of the content that was deemed as depicting natural events, even when the content had been moderated by a given platform. One participant, for example, identified a difference between a moderated video depicting "lions eating something" as opposed to "some vegan person has shared a video about an animal being tortured." However, even here, as will be discussed below, the reactions to these violent extreme examples were varied with one participant explaining how "personally I do watch the dogs abused in YouTube."

How Does Violent Extremist Material Make You Feel? What Does It Make You Do?

The 2018 survey captured young people's emotional and behavioural responses to online extreme content. The results of these two questions (Figures 4 and 5) drew attention to the gap between the expected or anticipated emotions and behaviours and those that were actually experienced by young people. This was of great assistance in helping us articulate the framework for the later in-depth focus groups.

The initial survey data captured a complexity of ways in which young people expressed their emotional responses to online violent extremist content. The list of possible emotions presented in the online survey arguably skewed responses towards negative emotions, particularly those that are frequently discussed in literature focused on the aims and objectives of violent extremism content producers. The most common emotions selected from the list were sad,

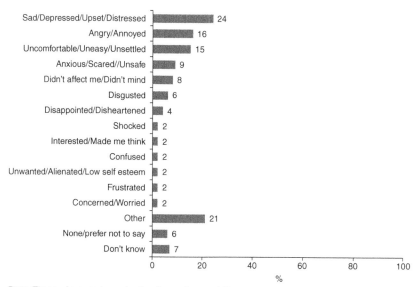

Base: Those who experienced extremism online n = 110
QB47: How did the extreme content you experienced make you feel?

Figure 4 How did the extreme content you experienced online make you feel?

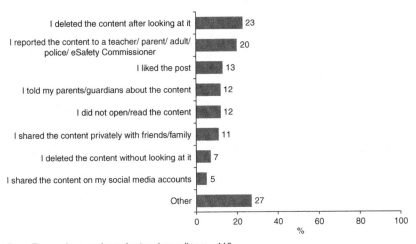

Base: Those who experienced extremism online n = 110
QB46: What did you do with the extreme content?

Figure 5 What did you do with the extreme content?

depressed, upset, and distressed (24 per cent). Despite this potential bias, the existence of a far broader and nuanced spectrum of emotions also emerged from the results. Young people reported that extreme content elicited anger and annoyance (9 per cent), an emotion that despite its negative associations has also been correlated with mobilisation and positive feelings (Waldek, Ballsun-Stanton, and Droogan 2020). Around one-fifth (21 per cent) of young people indicated that the emotions listed in the survey did not appropriately express their feelings, resulting in their selection of "other." This highlights the presence of a far more diverse spectrum of emotional responses to this content than was initially expected from a review of the terrorism literature.

When young people were asked about what they did with extreme content, the survey results again depicted a discrepancy between the behaviours anticipated by the survey creators and those actually performed by young people. The most common response from young people was that, after viewing the content, they would delete it (23 per cent) or report it to a teacher, parent, or adult or to the police or the eSafety Commissioner (20 per cent). Some of the respondents liked the content (13 per cent), shared it with friends and/or family (11 per cent), or shared it more broadly across social media platforms (5 per cent). However, once again the list of behaviours provided in the survey failed to include all the activities in which young people were actually engaging, with many respondents selecting "other" (27 per cent). The focus groups, as documented further in later sections, drew attention not just to the importance of placing the experiences of young people themselves at the centre of understanding of online violent extremist content. The groups also articulated the presence of a myriad of emotional and behavioural responses that may provide opportunities for increasing the resilience of young people to engage in an environment that is unlikely to ever be completely free from violent and extreme content.

3 The Diversity of Reactions to Online Violent Extremism

This section explores the emotional responses young people described in response to engaging with violent extremism, in particular on digital media. In it, we present a series of emotional responses to violent extremist content that often differ from the terror, fear, or shock that audiences are assumed to experience. Indeed, in addition to negative emotions young people reported a darkly humorous side of this material, its utility in rituals of bragging and rebellious performance, as well as a fundamental sense of curiosity. Many young people wrestled with fears about their exposure and had concerns about a poorly defined concept of desensitization. However, overall, it was the social context of this material, how they and their friends discussed and responded to it collectively and in relation to one another, that served to frame much of their discussions.

Concerns with sociality, with their friends, and to a lesser degree with family, infused the lives of the focus group participants. They couched their descriptions of online violent extremist content, as well as the minutiae of their lives, within the bounds of social relationships among peers, family members, educators, and the broader adult populations. As will be explored in more detail below, the emotions young people discussed in relation to online violent extremism often emerged within the context of a feedback loop of social validation. These emotional responses were affected by norms that young people perceived to operate within their peer groups and throughout wider society.

Cultivating an awareness of the social context of experiences of online violent extremist material highlights a disjuncture that has arisen from the moral panic associated with online violent extremism. Social concerns often focus on the media and technology as both the source of the problem and the location of the solution. However, as will be highlighted in this section, when we return our awareness to the critical social context of the media, the problem takes on a far more diverse and complex dimension. In turn, existing and new opportunities arise to build up resilience among young people and their social environments.

Sociality

Sociality is one of the most important qualities defining the complex relation-ships that shape and are shaped by the online environment. Digital media and their associated platforms, including social media (boyd and Ellison 2007), are predicated on human relationships. Digital media are proactively designed to enhance sociality through their ability to host, facilitate, and enhance social interactions (Marres and Gerlitz 2018; Nahon 2015).

The technological affordances of the multitude of social networking sites are not alone in crafting human emotional interactions with content and technology. As previously described in our definition of it, digital media's sociality is melded by humans whose behaviours and emotional responses are shaped by complex motivations, including identity construction and social relationships (Zhang and Leung 2015). Studies highlight the complex effects social media has on social connectedness and have shown both increases and decreases in social connectivity (Ryan et al. 2017; Ahn and Shin 2013; Grieve et al. 2013). It is unsurprising that violent, extreme content has an equally varied impact on young people.

Sociality and connectivity occur within an environment where, as has been well documented, the lived experience of an individual bridges the online and offline worlds. One participant in the focus group highlighted the fluidity between these environments when they stated: "Yeah. It's kind of like a conversation starter as well, which is weird, but it's – you definitely do talk about it offline moreover than online, I believe." It is this fusing of realities, often described in mainstream media and academia as distinct, that provides insight into the sense of penetration that digital media has had for young people. As another participant noted, digital media "is so woven into everybody's everyday lives."

This inherently social behaviour is paralleled in violent extremism. As the French anthropologist Scott Atran notes, "[P]eople don't simply kill and die for a cause. They kill and die for each other" (Atran 2011a, xi). That digital media has become a conduit for these social behaviours is hardly surprising. What is more complicated and far less understood, however, is what this shared mutual sociality means for individuals engaged in the production and consumption of its associated content, at both an emotional and a behavioural level. How are young people themselves navigating this sociality and its associations with identity formation as well as with the construction and sustenance of social relationships?

Research drawing on survey data examining young people's viewing of violent content (defined more broadly than extremism) documents the critical role played by social relationships, particularly those found within peer groups (Third et al. 2017). In parallel, terrorism scholarship has increasingly documented the key role social relationships play in processes of radicalisation to violent extremism (Nesser, Stenersen, and Oftedal 2016; Sageman 2008). Friendship groups generate pressures to engage in certain behaviours despite little real understanding of or deep resonance to the underpinning beliefs, values, and objectives, as was the case for several American Somalian young men who travelled together overseas to connect to the terrorist organisation Al Shabaab (Weine et al. 2009). The connection between sociality and violent extremism contributes to the associated fear that in this highly social online environment young people are particularly vulnerable. While it was clear that peer groups significantly impacted upon the experiences young people had with violent extremist content, any correlation with an associated vulnerability to radicalisation to violent extremism was far less clear. For example:

> [M]aybe I could say sending it to all my mates, sending – someone sending it to their mates, or my mates, and I'd just be – it'd be that – on their part, it'd be more showing off like look how brave I am, I guess.

Another participant stated:

> You kind of feel obligated to watch it as well. After watching these series, or videos, or pictures, you tell people straight away. Ooh my gosh, did you see that image or did you see that?

At the same time, the importance of understanding engagement with violent extremist content within a framework of sociality is highlighted by the role peer groups play in navigating and demarcating appropriate responses. These responses help to construct the boundaries of the in-group. Here the peer group represents a behavioural shibboleth that helps to determine the legitimacy of an individuals' membership in a community (Muniesa 2018), demarcating who is in and who is out. The following discussion, for example, describes how the participants' emotional responses were influenced by their peers:

Participant 1: Yeah, but it depends, because if you're in a big group, and the person who first reacts – the person who reacts to it first, is usually how everyone reacts to it as well . . . .
Participant 2: Yeah, that's true

In another encounter, a participant reiterated the active role peer groups play in creating the emotional boundaries around an individual's engagement with violent extremist content:

> It would depend on the context. If my friends were sending me a violent video or something either as a meme or as something to be horrified by, then I would probably adapt my response to their response. Otherwise you wouldn't really have much overreaction at all.

The conversations with participants consistently highlighted how their engagement with violent extremist content was framed within networks of sociality. These social relationships helped to moderate and mediate not only their behaviours, such as sharing content, but also their emotional engagement and responses. Young people documented a high degree of sensitivity to peer pressures. However, this pressure does not always result in vulnerabilities that increase the effectiveness of violent extremist content in "infecting" young minds. In contrast, the peer group also operated as a means of reinforcing the negative moral and normative framing of the content, something that may offer young people opportunities to strengthen their resilience to violent extremism.

Shock, Disbelief, Fear

The etymology of terrorism leaves no doubt that the emotion of terror is central to understanding how audiences are thought to respond to terrorist attacks. As Schmid has pointed out: "Terrorism is linked to terror which is a state of mind, created by a level of fear that so agitates body and mind that those struck by it are not capable of making an objective assessment of risks anymore" (2005, 137). This purposeful construction of fear and the idea that fear can be appropriately and effectively manipulated in various targeted audiences is a core feature of understanding terrorism as a strategy (Crawford 2013, 121).

The pivotal role played by fear in violent extremism makes it unsurprising that this emotion was frequently cited by the participants in conversations around their initial engagement with content. For example, when describing the viewing of a beheading video, one participant stated: "I remember seeing that and I was – at first, I just looked away and I couldn't watch it. I couldn't watch the guy getting his head sawed off. I was – I felt really – I felt a bit sick." Another participant describes how when seeing violent content relating to animal rights: "Sometimes you do get a little bit sad and tired I guess, but I guess mainly just shock and outrage." This expression of high negative emotions such as disgust, horror, and shock fits with wider research (Cantor 1998). In this quote a participant describes the emotions felt during the viewing of the Netflix documentary *Don't F**K with Cats*:

> So when he killed someone, it's – I mean, he already killed someone on the subway but he killed someone in his own house and that was the very – that really got to me. It kind of gave me nightmares. I felt shocked, surprised. At first, you will feel empathy for him because he was being bullied but at that time you say he's going overboard. All the things he does is – for – he's the only priority now ... so when I saw that, I was shocked and I – it was – I was speechless while watching that.

At times the fear expressed by participants was related to the perceived proximity or lack of proximity of the violent content. The nearer the violence was to their everyday experiences and communities the more fearful they felt in response to viewing the content online. For example:

> I think the closer to home, like where the video comes from, like the Christchurch shooting or the Lindt Café, I think the closer to home it is the more fear it puts in you. Because when you see something happening over in America, well that's all the way over in America, where these ones were closer to home. So I think they inflicted the most fear.

These expressions of negative emotions centred around the shock and fear generated by the viewing of violent online content align with research that, while focused on a slightly younger cohort (a survey of 25,142 nine-to-sixteen year olds) noted that the most commonly expressed emotional response to violent (although not necessarily extremist) content was fear or disgust (Livingstone et al. 2014). Given the association of these types of negative emotions with some of the psychological drivers towards engagement with violent extremism, it is unsurprising that the strong presence of negative feelings among young people also drives equally negative and fearful emotions in protective audiences such as parents, schools, and governments. Arguably, it is not only the presence of fear and related emotions that helps to shape the deeply concerned and even panicked responses. These responses are also driven by a pervading sense of a lack of control these same audiences have (or perceive themselves to have) over the online environment. This may be because a lack of control is central to fear (Nabi 2010).

This relationship between violence and terror has led to an institutionalization of the centrality of negative emotions such as fear, anger, and anxiety in terrorism studies predating even the attacks of September 11. (Crawford 2000). Yet, treating the relationship between violent extremist content and emotions as a series of biologically determined reactions misses the way in which an individual's emotions are generated through a far broader and more dynamic process (Wright-Neville and Smith 2009). It situates the encounter solely within the domain of feelings as opposed to the more complex role emotions play as producers of effects and behaviours, both negative and positive. This complexity was expressed by respondents who frequently caveated the initial expression of fear and other negative emotions with references to other types of feelings.

The Christchurch attack case study outlined in the introduction is an example of the complexity of emotional responses to online violent extremism. The participant quoted in our introduction initially expressed shock and horror at the appropriation of what he identified as "his" online culture by the Christchurch attacker, noting how "it ruined the humour behind the subscribe to PewDiePie. After that moment . . . those jokes just weren't really funny at all." Yet he later noted that despite the generation of negative emotions he was still engaged in the culture, stating "but obviously, I'm still into it, so, yeah, I was like woah."

Here, the shock generates the type of evaluation that Sara Ahmed describes in her work on the affective nature of emotions, whereby the initial reaction causes a type of self-reflection that can be evaluative in nature (Ahmed 2014). In this case, the initial horror of the appropriation of their online culture for purposes of real-world and livestreamed violent extremism caused the participant's ongoing enjoyment of the culture to include a parallel sense of unease and disquiet.

While the shock, disbelief, and other negative emotions experienced by young people should clearly remain an integral part of any investigation of online violent extremism, the above examples point to a much-needed problematisation of any simple conclusion that starts and ends with just the emotion of terror. It is more useful to perceive these types of emotions as the starting point of an examination of the dynamic, nuanced, and often ambiguous lived experience of young people who, in their own words, are frequently exposed to and engaged with such content, online and offline.

Curiosity

The sensation of curiosity is familiar in daily life, yet it was surprising to many of the participants that they experienced curiosity in response to online violent extremist content. The following exchanges are good examples of how curiosity was often initially discussed:

Participant 1: I feel disgusted
Participant 2: I feel that as well but ooh my god, I hate to say this but I kind of feel curious as well.

And:

> I get a sense of curiosity because it's not something I see every day. So it's shocking and it's like you get curious at what this is and – because it's not common to see.

Given this forbidden yet ubiquitous content, it is hardly surprising that almost all participants expressed curiosity, an emotion centred on the desire for information (Hsee and Ruan, 2016). Empirical research has demonstrated how morbid curiosity generates behaviours that lead humans to deliberately view and engage with negative content, including death, violence, and gore (Niehoff and Oosterwijk 2020; Scrivner 2020). This morbid curiosity was described by a participant who stated that:

> I think there's like a, kind of like a morbid curiosity about it. Like you kind of want to see what's on the other side but it might not exactly be something that you want to see. It's just like you're kind of compelled to see it.

Curiosity can be experienced both positively and negatively. So, while for some participants it is likely that the taboo nature of the content triggered curiosity, others described a more positive process of knowledge acquisition. Here the participants seem to experience curiosity in relation to a desire to learn more about the context, background, or nature of the thing represented by the violent extremist content. In a study of adolescents in high school (Jovanovic and Brdaric 2012), higher levels of the trait of curiosity were linked with higher levels of life satisfaction and positive well-being, raising questions around the possible value of this emotional trait for the resilience of young people with regard to their experience and consumption of violent extremist content. As one participant expressed: "Sometimes curiosity is the driving force for you to see things because you want to know what's happening." Curiosity highlights the disjuncture between the moral panic, the aims of moderation or restriction, and the experiences of young people around the use of such content as a means of fulfilling inquisitive and entertainment needs. As another participant noted: "[Us] young people want to know more about these violent acts, like what's going in their head. What's making them do this, was it their childhood? That's what makes us curious about these videos."

The attractive power of curiosity raises a concern that social media regulators, in making it more difficult to find and acquire moderated content, may contribute to the movement of young people into more niche platforms where, ironically, exposure to violent extremist content is not only more likely but the social space of exposure is also potentially more extreme.

The presence of positive and negative expressions of curiosity reflects the complexity of emotions when interacting with online violent extremism. Curiosity can emerge from deprivation whereby the individual has a strong but unsatisfied need to acquire information, as well as from interest, whereby the individual is seeking out information for the sensation of pleasure (Litman and Jimerson, 2004). So, while we saw this ongoing desire to learn more, we saw equally that participants coupled their curiosity with an acknowledgement of not only the humorous elements of the content but also the sociality of engagement and the associated enjoyment and satisfaction that comes from such connectivity.

Another interesting connection to curiosity emerged from discussions with participants on reporting content to social media platforms and the moderation undertaken by such companies. These discussions often focused primarily on

Facebook and its approach to moderation wherein violent content is hidden and users are given a written warning statement and required to actively click to reveal the content. Repeatedly participants described how they "get tempted to click and look, just because it's hidden. It's like you're curious. It raises your curiosity."

It was not uncommon for participants to report that a moderation process generated a desire to obtain the information, to expose themselves to the content to learn about it, and to fill the knowledge gap. For example:

> On Facebook ... they usually censor – ask – if content's going to be very violent and whatnot, usually young people will just press okay, and straight away the video appears. It's shocking. You know what you're going to see but you still want to see it, I guess. Do you know what I mean?

These experiences raise questions about the objectives of moderating techniques that focus on the provision of warning statements and reduced initial visibility of the violent content. Humans will repeatedly seek to resolve perceived uncertainty even when there is an expectation of negative consequences (Hsee and Ruan 2016).

As one participant noted, even after viewing a warning sign on Instagram: "I still click it." By removing the content temporarily and placing a warning that indicates a knowledge gap, these techniques are perhaps more likely to engage the user and result in the consumption of the violent content. For example, one participant noted how the presence of warning statements made them less likely to go on to report the content as "if you report it, you're hypocritical because I do agree to watching this, if it affects me then it's my own fault ... because Facebook has warned me."

This raises questions about the objectives of moderation strategies. Should moderation be about providing an individual with agency in their consumption of specific types of material or is moderation focused on restricting opportunities for engagement with such content? These objectives are important, especially when we consider the unintended consequences these techniques might have on the likelihood of individuals reporting the content (and other such content) once they have actively engaged in its consumption.

Humour

Humour was a recurrent, if limited, theme raised by young people across the focus groups. A few participants talked about sometimes finding online violent and extreme content funny, about sharing it with peers because of its humour and shock value, and about using black humour as a coping mechanism when exposed to difficult online materials. This was particularly the case when they were discussing violent and extreme content in a group, at which time humour became a way of demonstrating bravado to peers.

That online violent extremist content can be darkly humorous should come as no surprise to anyone familiar with the meme culture generated by Islamic State and its fans, or with the ironic trolling that permeates far-right culture online. The 2019 Christchurch attack demonstrated a worrying confluence of terrorism and entertainment. In it, violence was stylised to entertain a community of online trolls, while simultaneously the perpetrator's use of humour and irony became a hook to entrance those vulnerable to indoctrination to the underlying white supremacist message. According to one analyst (Johnston 2019):

> In this form of terrorism, radicalisation takes place under a veneer of entertainment and humour plays an important role in desensitising the viewer to the horror of what is being portrayed. The fact that real human beings are being killed is concealed by euphemistic memes and grand narratives of cultural conflict.

This has led to fears among concerned media, policy makers, and academics that the online use of humour in combination with violent extremist content, even during livestreamed attacks, may serve to "open the door to a competition of one-upmanship between online figures seeking to "outperform" their fellows in terms of the gore, dark humour, and obscenity of the content they produce" (Johnston 2019). Even a cursory review of some of the far-right forums on social media platforms such as 4chan or 8kun provides ample evidence for this cynical and ironically humorous game of one-upmanship between members.

Certainly, the use of humour is a potent way to make violent extremist memes and messages appealing enough to become viral and spread horizontally among peers, and noteworthy enough to be discussed and dissected afterwards and remembered years later. However, our research suggests that young people have a relatively sophisticated awareness of the roles humour plays in online extremist material. They demonstrated an awareness of the reasons why humour is used in this cynical way by content creators. In particular, respondents showed they recognised that violent extremist content is often designed to be funny as a way to attract their attention and to encourage shares.

For example, interviewees discussed violent gore clips of explicit traffic accidents that were purposefully edited to be darkly funny through the addition of club music as backing track. Or, more notoriously, they recalled the infamous Islamic State Peppa Pig video clips in which excerpts from the popular toddler's television cartoon were edited to both shock and entertain. In these, Peppa and her animated animal friends suddenly and unexpectedly switch from their toddler-friendly cartoon antics to firing automatic weapons and yelling Islamic State slogans in Arabic, all to the backing of a popular and menacing Islamic State chant (*nasheed*). These were said to be simultaneously scary and funny, possibly due to the juxtaposition of the innocent nostalgia of childhood with the foreign and violent sloganeering of Islamic State terrorists.

Participant 1: There were – it was a while back I think, maybe last year, the Peppa Pig videos
Participant 2: Ooh yeah.
Participant 3: Yeah that was just a bit scary
Facilitator: You're laughing?
Participant 1: I'm laughing at it now but . . .

This confluence of humour and shock value creates an enabling environment in which violent extremist content is more likely to be spread virally online (Waldek, Ballsun-Stanton, and Droogan 2020). Young people are aware of this dynamic. Their peers share content because it's funny, and it's funny primarily because it's shocking. Indeed, this process by which the violent or extremist message becomes secondary, even irrelevant, compared to the humour and shock value is understood, even if this understanding does not necessarily prevent young people from continuing to share the material. This, of course, is exactly what the content creators want them to do.

Participant 1: . . . it gets the views and stuff it's because look how crazy this is and then sort of disappears but your view stacks onto everyone else's and then it becomes – like everyone gets to see it.
Participant 2: It's primarily for the humour/shock value. There's only a . . .
Participant 1: Yeah.
Participant 2: . . . very select number of people actually share it for the gory content in the first place. Yeah 100 per cent.

Sharing funny content or memes with peers can also be a way of showing off and gaining credibility in social circles where novel online content that is shocking and funny is a primary currency of value. This is not because viewers have any desire to spread extremist propaganda, but instead they want to show off and one-up their mates. In this regard, one of the respondents claimed they shared humorous violent and extreme content because: "It'd be more showing off like look how brave I am, I guess."

During our discussions with young people some of them raised this dynamic, demonstrating they were aware that sharing funny clips had a darker purpose, and that they had to be careful which of their mates they included. Some of the males in particular projected an attitude of sophisticated confidence that they could outwit terrorists because they know who among their friends could handle the difficult material and who couldn't:

> I rarely share that type of content. I only share it if they really want to see it, but I make sure that it's not like here you go, just watch it, it's funny. I just make sure I go this is a video, are you sure you want to watch it? They're like yeah and it's like okay. But the people I share [unclear] they're my close friends, I'll know if something's up with them after they watch that, they become radicalised or whatever. I'll know there's something up with them.

In these social contexts it can be difficult for young people to escape exposure to widely shared materials, particularly when what they're sharing is "just a joke." Peer pressure, however, means that disengagement may be preferable to speaking out to their peers about their discomfort with the violent material. One respondent articulated their confidence in extracting themselves from a social set in which the confluence of violent extremism and dark humour had become popular:

> I was in a group of friends exactly like he was, with dark humour, but I never really contributed to it because I personally, whenever I see a dead body I just freak out. So whenever they shared it or spoke about it in class, that's when I would distance myself, because I just personally feel really freaked out by it. But I never obviously pulled them up on any of it, I just don't participate but I don't say anything about it either, if that makes sense.

Importantly, humour is not simply a Trojan horse through which violent extremist materials are inserted into youth culture. Humour can also be a factor in how violent extremist materials are discussed and digested among peers after viewing. Yet, rather than providing a pathway to deeper or more engaging discussions about the content, its creators, or effects, the humour was usually explained as a shallow way of dismissing the more serious and profound aspects of the material. In particular, larger groups were described as taking a lead from peers who focus on the humorous aspects of the posts instead of really engaging with its difficult violent content or messaging.

> If someone says ooh that's funny, everyone's like yeah that's funny, or if someone says ooh wow, that's really … who would do that, and everyone would go deep. It just really depends on how big the group is.

This collective response among peers dismissing material as merely funny is contrasted with an understanding that in a more personal or intimate social setting the humour may in fact be a strategy for coping with difficult content. According to one respondent: "I think the laughing and the humour, some people use it as a coping mechanism to try and get through all this sadness … it's just so much that maybe you use it just to cope." This reiterates the importance of examining these interactions and ultimately the consumption and engagement with such content through a lens of sociality.

Along with concerns about desensitization, some young respondents were anxious about their ability to find online violent extremist material humorous or ironic, and their seeming inability to "take anything seriously." In this regard, their humour was described as providing a form of protection from the difficult realities that sit behind violent and extreme content, a way of making it acceptable and thus also dismissible.

Participant 1: We don't really take anything seriously. When we were in high school, extremists were like blood and all these things now, but nowadays it's kind of a joke.
Participant 2: Yeah, they incorporate it into humour . . ..
Participant 3: Yeah.
Participant 4: It just makes it feel like it's acceptable because it's humour.
Participant 5: Mm-hm. I think it's also how we cope with it as well.
Participant 6: Yeah.

However, an understanding of the violent and extremist realities of the content, and the real-world negative emotions and effects that it can trigger, does at times surface. When it does, this tension between laughter and tragedy can be difficult to negotiate by young people, and can put pressure on their social relationships. One respondent, who was obviously proud of their dark humour and world-weary, jaded attitude to online violent extremist material, described the difficulties that emerged when the "humour" of the Christchurch livestream attack met the lived reality of human tragedy:

> I have dark humour . . .. There was one point where one of my mates – like a Kiwi mate and then when the Christchurch thing happened, one of my other mates made a joke about it. Then that's when I tried to reconsider my type of humour, because my Kiwi friend got really upset, not angry but just upset. It made me reevaluate, is this – should I be openly laughing about these jokes or whatever?

The confluence of humour and online violent extremism, and even of entertainment and terrorism, has recently become a significant issue in relation to online far-right extremist movements and groups. Humour and irony has been used by the far right to camouflage their extremism and tacit support for violence in a fashion that makes their violent extremist ideology and aims deniable (Weimann and Ben Am 2020). This poses a problem for effective counter-terrorism programs because of the attractive and positive emotions humour generates even when concealing a more dangerous agenda.

Ironically, the use of humour to conceal a darker extremist message is the direct reverse of a strategy of employing humour to counter terrorist narratives. For instance, satire and humour that pokes fun at serious and grave terrorists has been shown to have the ability to reach large numbers of people and to act as a popular and grassroots counter narrative to the fear promulgated by extremists and their violence. Studies have shown that well-targeted humour can act as a form of cultural resistance to acts of terrorism and the ideologies they propagate (Stephan 2015), and can empower populations impacted by terrorism by offering them an avenue through which they can vent negative emotions in a prosocial way (Al-Rawi 2016).

Comics in Muslim majority nations, for instance, have used these strategies to good effect against Islamic State and in particular its serious and grandiose claims to represent true Islam and the political future of the global *ummah*. In the online domain, for example, satirical Twitter accounts have been created posting footage of Islamic State cadres dubbed with popular love songs instead of the usual militant chants (Stephan 2015). Alternatively, satire has been successfully used as a strategy in television shows such as *Halal in the Family* in order to confront negative terrorist-related stereotypes about Muslims in the United States, and thus to counter Islamophobic and far-right narratives that conflate Islam with terrorism (Miles 2015).

Such grassroots satire ridicules and undermines the false authority and fear projected by groups such as Islamic State in a visceral and immediate fashion, transforming fear into laughter and providing a social outlet for free and positive anti-terrorist discussions. When online, this content can directly engage with very difficult and sensitive issues in a way that is accessible to the public and that bypasses state control or censorship (Tang 2013). In sum, the use of humour provides an authentic, accessible, positive emotional response to the horrors of violent extremism. That said, humour is also very effective at masking violent and extremist materials through the adding a veneer of positive emotional experience to content. This allows material to be shared freely as jokes among peers who consume and share it for its humour as well as its shock value.

Attention, Bragging, Rebelliousness

An attraction to online violent extremist material due to its shock value and the bragging rights this conveys onto those who post or share it with peers was a recurrent, if limited, theme among participants in the focus groups. Both males and females reported sometimes being attracted to violent and extreme posts, particularly humorous ones, because of their inherent subversiveness and the appeal this has for those wanting to appear rebellious. According to one respondent:

> [Y]ou're talking in the group chat and then someone sends a video of something really messed up and it's just funny. It's sort of funny because

picture if we're all having a conversation about the party you went to and someone gets a computer screen, a laptop, puts some ISIS beheading and then slaps it in the middle of the table. We're like oh. Think about it on a personal scale. That's why – then that person, it's just – maybe it gives them that glimmer of attention? Respect? All that.

In this example, casually bombing a party or group chat with a hyper-violent clip is considered darkly humorous, a sudden comedic non-sequitur that can grant the poster attention, respect, and acclaim because it transgresses accepted social norms.

This attraction to extreme material because of its transgressive value and the esteem that it can bestow upon those who share it with friends may occur simply because of how novel and unique the material is. Effectively, this fascination may be no more significant than a desire to "look at this crazy stuff" with friends. As one participant described:

> [I]f you click on some random, say international Facebook page, that posts funny content, like you'll scroll down and you end up on just some completely violent extremist – potentially not every single time but you'd just end up on that and then because that's such a small random group, you can send it to a friend . . . and you'll just be like have a look at this, look how crazy it is and it's sort of like it's not the fact that oh we love looking at this kind of crazy stuff, it's more or less like as it's on Facebook, look at this crazy stuff, you know what I mean?

However, this attraction to extreme and transgressive content, and the one-upmanship that can result among friends when they compete with one another to see and share every example of more extreme material, can lead to a process of escalation. In this case, young people report initially consuming and sharing violent and extreme content because of its novelty and the credibility it bestows on them among friends, but eventually reaching a point where they can no longer ignore the effect this exposure is having on them. For example:

> [T]here is an instance of where I did see a video and I was like – so like I have a high tolerance with sort of, I don't know, gore or whatever you want to say in like extremist videos on Facebook whatever, but then there's just like this example of one video and it was like, it was quite extreme, I'm not going to lie. It was a very extreme video. But the amount that it was spoken to was sort of sit around with friends and then oh look at this crazy video we saw on Facebook. Then the question would come, and it'd be like what's the craziest stuff you've seen? Like what's the craziest whatever you want to say, like – what's the worst thing you've seen? What's the craziest? I was like that one is stuck, you know what I mean? That one stuck. Like it doesn't impact me day to day, but it was like I didn't really need to see that. I sort of got too curious and then saw it, but I was like, I didn't really need to see that.

Violent and extreme material may be attractive to young people because of its transgressive and subversive content and the credibility that association with the material may convey among peers. Certainly, terrorists and violent extremists have long acknowledged a desire to capture and exploit the rebelliousness of youth to their cause. The very act of terrorism as a visceral and immediate propaganda of deeds instead of words was originally used by the nineteenth century anarchists in Europe to directly inspire potential radicals. In the 1960s leftist- and Marxist-inspired terror groups operating in Western Europe and the United States, such as the Baader-Meinhof Gang, attracted counter-culture youth motivated by a passion to subvert the "system" and bring about a global anti-capitalist revolution (von Stetten 2009). More recently, the so-called Islamic State has gone to great lengths to "motivate crowds drawn from the masses to fly to the regions which we manage, particularly the youth. [For] the youth of the nations are closer to the innate nature [of humans] on account of the rebelliousness within them" (Atran 2015).

This quote is taken from the notorious *Management of Savagery*, an online manual produced in Iraq in the mid-2000s as a map for successfully waging global terrorist jihad. It was later adopted by Islamic State as a blueprint for its caliphate-building project (Naji et al. 2006). Following its advice, Islamic State expended significant resources to produce a vast array of slick and sophisticated online propaganda to make their movement appear hip and to motivate youth to join them. In so doing they ruthlessly exploited youthful passion, idealism, and a quest for significance, as well as their "innate" rebelliousness as well (Droogan and Peattie 2017).

However, this youthful rebellious character may be less innate than Islamic State and other extremist groups wish. During focus groups, young people talked less about being attracted to extremist material because it fulfilled a pre-existing desire to be rebellious, and more about using the material with peers in a humorous way in order to cultivate a popular transgressive persona. For instance:

> The stuff they send me, just the shock, you're expected to be shocked at it. When I was a kid, I thought it would be cool to be the exact opposite, because it just shows I'm going against the expectations. Maybe that would be funnier, that I was not shocked at it, but that's when I was a kid.

Young men in particular discussed how an ability to consume and share violent and difficult material online among friends was considered to be a desirable trait. It was something that boys did among themselves as a form of bragging, or with girls in order to demonstrate their transgressive credibility. Young women, however, were at times aware of this dynamic and pointed out how boys they knew related to violent extremist materials in a competitive way with their mates, and how this was quite different to from their own interactions with other females:

Participant 1: I think sometimes they pretend they don't care . . .
Participant 2: . . . because of what they're supposed to feel I guess.
Participant 1: Mm-hm. They want to seem manly, like they've seen worse, like ooh nah, I've seen this other video that's even worse. They kind of – yeah, they kind of compete with what they've seen which is not how we would talk about it at all.

In these examples we can see how online violent and extremist material is being used by young people in order to strengthen and reinforce their bonds with friends, or perhaps to gain the attention of people they want to attract sexually. In this case, extremist materials can be used to create an interlinked community (either online, offline, or both) that share a common set of values that set them apart from the mainstream (Atran 2011b). Violent extremist materials may be sought, consumed, shared, and discussed in a way that does not necessarily denote any real affinity with the underlying political or religious ideology, but instead creates social bonds. The violent extremist videos, clips, memes, and images may signify the creation of a rebellious tribal counter-culture among groups of friends, but not necessarily one that is approving of actual extremism or violence.

Desensitization

Participants in the focus groups frequently brought up and discussed the term "desensitization" to describe an anxiety they felt about their emotional responses to online violent extremist material. Although there are relatively few studies examining processes of desensitization in relation to digital media and terrorism, wider literature looking at legacy mass media helps contextualise what young people mean when they talk about desensitization.

Research into the impact that exposure or consumption of media violence may have on young people's social behaviour has often drawn upon the general aggression model – a metatheory that posits how exposure to media violence influences a process of desensitization – in contrast to the therapeutic use of desensitization to reduce cognitive and emotional responses to an unwanted or negative emotion or behaviour (Brewin 1996). Exposure to violent media causes this process of desensitization to become associated with a reduction in the cognitive and emotional responses of the individual (DeLisi et al. 2013). Carnagey et al., in their study on video games, argue that desensitization occurs because the violence is presented in a positive way which may reduce the distressing reactions to such content and in the long term may reduce the sympathy felt for the victims (Carnagey, Anderson, and Bartholow 2007). While the Carnagey study, as is the case with much of the empirical research into desensitization and violent media, does not consider social media, similar positive packaging of violent content is often seen in extremist content. The viewing of violent media, it is therefore argued, reduces an individual's perception of fear and anxiety of the material influencing future responses, for example, a reduced emotional reactivity, a decreased empathy for the victim, and an increase in antisocial or aggressive behaviours (Mrug et al. 2015; DeLisi et al. 2013).

As noted, while there are still relatively few studies examining processes of desensitization specifically in relation to online social media content, participants in the focus groups themselves frequently drew on the term desensitization to describe their emotional responses to online violent extremist content over time or described an emotional process that resembles that encompassed by the term. For example:

> I think because of the amount and frequency of it now, we've almost become desensitized to it. So, it doesn't leave as much as a lasting impression once you see it. The first time obviously it's a bit shocking . . .. But after seeing it tens and hundreds of times your brain builds up just a filter to it and kind of doesn't get to you as much as it would if you were seeing it for the first time. So, you become really desensitized to it I guess.

Another participant noted:

> Yeah, I guess it helps to just soldier on to the next day. It sort of builds up – I don't know if that's the right term, but it builds up an immunity towards it. Just if my friends want to show me some more, I won't be as shocked. I'll just go whatever.

The emotional responsiveness of young people, including empathy and sympathy, has also been linked to their moral development and social behaviour (Vossen and Fikkers 2020). This connectivity has likely impacted what has become a highly contentious, polarised, and political debate around the influence of violent media on emotional responsiveness and by association the development of morality and social behaviour of young people (Funk et al. 2004). Increasingly, scholars are pointing to a more complex reading of the empirical evidence that highlights the presence of a multi-causal relationship and a need for a more nuanced understanding of the points of correlation and causation (Prot and Gentile 2014), as was reflected in the discussions that emerged in the focus groups.

Alongside the descriptions of a numbing towards online violent extremist content, participants also described parallel and alternative responses to the same content. These responses often highlighted the possible role played by temporality and geolocation in relation to online violent extremist content. There was a sense among some participants that the fact the violence was occurring far away in another country, or place, or at another time point, reduced its impact. For example:

> I know this sounds maybe slightly extreme, but I just sort of remind myself that I am in a very privileged situation to be living in this country and that I'm living in a sort of culture where I don't have things happen to me . . . .. But also, at the same time, I don't know, maybe it's because I'm not aware of the effects, but when you're watching it there's an immediate disconnect from it because it's on a screen, if you know what I mean. You're not there in real life. It would be much more traumatic seeing people out there.

This sense of a distinction between reality and fiction is raised by the following participant in their discussion of their viewing of the Christchurch terrorist attack through the Facebook Live feed, whereby they highlight a difference in their emotional response because of the sense they had of the reality and immediacy of the violence:

> I think with those execution videos I watched when I was a kid, it was more like they only showed a before and after. They didn't show the actual beheading . . . .. [W]ith the Christchurch video, it's like you see people begging for their lives, you can see them begging for mercy while you can see the guy actually shooting . . . they didn't sign up for it, in a way, the people getting executed.

Equally, for some participants there was a sense that the knowledge gleaned from social media (its educational capacity) and the fictionality associated with video gaming diminished its influence on their behaviour:

> I feel like personally from what I've heard, it comes back to the argument about violent video games cause children to be violent and I completely don't think that's the case because if you think about it watching a violent video of someone in somewhere else doing whatever, you just can't – you're way more – you're not attached to that. But if you're playing a video game and you're simulating whatever and you have the controls, I can understand why that would put someone in a position where yeah maybe they have the control and they enjoy doing this. But at the end of the day it's definitely not the case.

One of the greatest differences noted by participants between their perceived desensitization from repeated exposure to online violent extremist content occurred in movement between the online and offline spaces. During the discussions, several participants described how their experiences with violent extremism had not prepared or inured them from strong emotional responses when encountering violence in the real world:

> [B]ut I remember ... I saw a hard-core fight, I was – a street fight were two people are actually trying to kill each other, I was like woah and the desensitize – the media I've watched before did not do much to desensitize what it was like in real life for me.

Another participant reflected on this disjunction between mediated and unmediated experiences of extremism and violence:

> It's [online violent extremism] made out so dramatic, I guess in media, films and TV shows. Then when you actually see something horrific in real life it's like like oh, that's it? It's a lot quieter than I thought it would be.

One young person noted how their online engagement had not prevented them from intervening in a real fight: "Yeah, so I was definitely – I wasn't desensitized to it because if that was the case, I wouldn't have done anything, I think. At all. I wouldn't have had that instinct to get up and help."

These discussions parallel the complexity found in the research around the influence desensitization has on behaviours such as empathy and sympathy in relation to violent media over time, although it should be noted the research does not look at a distinction between online and offline incidents of violence (Vossen and Fikkers 2020). Desensitization represents an important perceived emotional response among the participants. However, its behavioural associations are not always those of disengagement, particularly in the real world. This finding highlights a gap in understanding on the role desensitization may have on processes of radicalisation and resilience towards violent extremism.

4 Strategies of Engagement

During the focus groups it became increasingly clear participants exhibited a broad spectrum of behaviours following their exposure to online violent extremist content. In part, this reflected the limits content producers themselves face in effectively eliciting specific emotions from the design and placement of content. It also emerged from the intersection of individual identities, experiences, and interests with the medial and generic technological characteristics of online environments (Eder 2018).

Within this complex environment, the participants did not emerge as passive observers forced to engage with an endless stream of violent extremist content. Participants not only vocalised a variety of behaviours but often coupled these with an articulation of the decision-making behind the selection and expectations of emotional consequences. These problem-solving strategies can be usefully framed through Nahon's prism of curation. Curation is described as a process whereby "participants repeatedly demonstrate an ability to select and organise, to filter abundance into a collection of manageable size, to search, reframe and remix" (Nahon 2015, 20).

The demonstrated ability of participants to curate their experiences online are indicative of some degree of resilience (Vandoninck, d'Haenens, and Roe 2013, 62), a term that has recently gained wide currency in the field of terrorism research. The presence and articulation of a wide variety of behavioural strategies, which are used by participants in relation to content classified as violent extremist, support wider findings on resilience where it is defined as "the ability to thrive in contexts of adversity or challenge through positive, prosocial adaptation; the presence and mobilization of protective factors that can offset risks and vulnerabilities, and the ability to access and navigate resources in culturally meaningful ways" (Grossman et al. 2020, 3).

The encounters presented in this section do not suggest that young people are necessarily resilient enough to confidently navigate the extremes of terrorist content online. However, in contrast to the imaginings conjured up by concerned adult communities, these encounters do document a wide variety of existing strategies, resources, and opportunities that are drawn upon by young people to curate their way through emotionally complex and at times violent environments. Rather than detail each strategy depicted by members of the focus groups, we have selected some of the more commonly discussed behaviours as illustrative of this process of curation. We use them to indicate the remarkable diversity of curative possibilities embedded within young people's engagement with online violent extremist content.

Scrolling and Ignoring

One approach described by participants that appears at first glance relatively simple on the surface was simply to ignore difficult, violent, and extreme content. For example:

> So most of the time I personally tend to just ignore it because there's not much I can do since it's being shared so many times and it's also partly informational. Like it's still news. It's just, it just so happened it's violent and graphic.

However, on further examination a series of associated behaviours emerge. One such behaviour is scrolling. For instance, one participant stated: "When I was browsing Facebook, sometimes it [violent extremist content] will just be on the platform. When it's violent, I'll just scroll and I won't watch it." Another noted that: "If I see something incredibly bad online, I see it and I just keep moving. I don't really focus too much on it."

Scrolling is a behaviour that has been cultivated and embedded into all of our day-to-day online curation activities. It reflects the business models of many social media platforms whose aim and business model are focused on keeping users engaged on their platforms for an extended period. It has been described as a core part of the "liveness" of social media, scrolling is a quality that has contributed to the sense of "drowning in an endless informational flow" described by commentators and social media users alike (Lupinacci 2020, 13–14). While the process of scrolling through content represents a relatively normal strategy, it has also been described as part of a series of behaviours associated with coping strategies employed by young people in response to traumatic or uncomfortable online content. Using scrolling in this way reflects passive coping – exhibiting behaviour that either denies or ignores the stressor (Carver, Scheier, and Weintraub 1989).

Very few participants described deleting violent or extreme content, describing instead how they moved through it quickly or moved away from the content. This is likely to reflect the technological affordances of popular platforms such as Instagram, Snapchat, and Facebook where it is not possible to directly delete content posted by others. References to deletion as a means of minimising and reducing exposure to violent extremist content usually occurred in relation to direct messaging apps such as WhatsApp. For example: "In WhatsApp groups like maybe some extremist videos of like ISIS beheading people. But I mean the moment I see what it is I just delete it because I really don't want to see people being beheaded."

Other behaviours reflect more proactive behaviours such as blocking content and users or restricting opportunities to encounter violent extremist content by unfollowing:

> I used to follow this account. I don't know, it used to be something different but then they sort of receive all of these different videos . . .. So there were a lot of graphic videos of animals being hurt or slaughtered and it just got to a point where I just couldn't follow it anymore, so I just unfollowed them.

This highlights the decision-making strategies involved in selecting from the different blocking behaviours available to participants. The users' behaviour is impacted on perceived social connectivity to the poster/producer of content, whereby unfollowing reduces exposure while maintaining a façade to the poster/producer of ongoing receptivity and "engaged friendship" from the user/receiver:

> For me, if I don't know the one who posts it, I would block them so that I won't be able to see those kinds of posts again. If the one who posted is a friend or someone I know, I'll just unfollow them so I won't be seeing them on my timeline but they're still [my friends].

The presence of both passive and active coping strategies has been associated with a degree of pre-existing trauma and anxiety among young audiences (Christine et al. 2018). The participants, however, at times associated the agency involved in these types of behaviours with emotions of relief: "I had to block someone because they kept posting pictures of foetuses . . .. It was a relief not to be confronted with that every second day."

The conscious decisions to block or unfollow individuals often occurred within a broader set of behaviours. These suggest that in the generation of curative engagements on social media young people express a degree of learned and adaptive behaviours beyond just passive denial of the content. This example also suggests an awareness, as detailed in Section 5, among some of the participants about the objectives of content producers; that is to maximise exposure through users spreading shocking material through their online networks. One participant noted that:

> I think whenever you see something that's shocking you feel the urge to share it and so I find it's better to vocally tell someone oh, look at this video before blocking and reporting and all that sort of stuff, rather than sharing on the digital platform because you're not really – you're trying not to spread it but then you're also getting that load off your chest and being like look, this is disgusting, without promoting it in any way.

Sharing

Content is disseminated across the Internet through sharing behaviours facilitated by the various technological affordances of platforms that allow users to reproduce and share content among their social networks and beyond, both privately and publicly. There was little evidence of impulsive sharing demonstrated during the focus groups. Most participants reported that they thought before posting. The ubiquity of sharing, however, cultivated a sense of acceptability and normality around the decisions made to disseminate violent extremist content, as described by the following participant: "It's like everyone has done it so you feel it's fine for you to share it."

These norms also allow participants to learn more about appropriate behaviours and emotions in response to given content (boyd 2015). In doing so the behaviour allows them to cultivate their own sense of identity and interconnectivity in given social networks. These processes of identity formation reflect research that argues public acts of sharing require considerable social investment as individuals are revealing to their peers (and imagined communities) a sense of what is important to them (Lane and Dal Cin 2018):

Again, with sharing, when you see those memes and see those funny videos we instantly share or tell people offline what they've seen. Have you seen this meme? That would relate to another meme that looks similar.

Another noted that:

[M]aybe I could say sending it to all my mates, sending – someone sending it to their mates, or my mates, and I'd just be – it'd be that – on their part, it'd be more showing off like look how brave I am, I guess.

Sharing content has also been shown to fulfil a range of emotional purposes. For instance, sharing content helps to generate deeper understandings for the user and recipient about the spectrum of acceptable reactions and feelings (Berger and Milkman 2012). This was clear from a number of participants' responses; as one stated:

[I] kind of feel better, just knowing that they see the wrong as well. Yeah, that's another reason why everyone shares, just so you can see the shared feelings of this dehumanised video.

This sense of catharsis however has been shown to have little long-term impact on the initial emotional memory associated with content, suggesting a degree of fragility embedded with this curative strategy (Rimé 2009). Given the central role sociality and social relationships appear to play in the process of radicalisation to violent extremism (see, for example, work by Sageman 2008; Malthaner and Waldmann 2014), this fragility around emotional memory reiterates the need to better understand young people's navigation of the interplay between emotions and specific digital qualities such as sharing, sociality, and online violent extremist content. How and when do these behaviours transform from protective qualities to areas of concern in relation to violent extremism?

Participants also documented how the act of sharing allowed them to inform and educate others about specific issues or events that they perceived as important and relevant. These perceived responsibilities as well as moral and ethical concerns reflect research that shows how teenagers' online behaviours display moral sensitivity and empathic concern for how those they are socially connected with may be negatively affected by the material (Flores and James 2013). On young person noted that:

Personally, I do watch the dogs abused in the YouTube [videos]. It's not because I like the dogs being abused, but I just want to know more about what the dogs are being treated now. Sometimes I send those videos to my friends because I want them to know about the animal abuse problems.

Another that:

> These videos that we see, it kind of unites people as well. I think that's another reason why people share it, to remember those people who were murdered or hurt. We see people, just the Muslims, we see they're hurt, their community was killed, it's something that everyone can kind of – not relate to but show love.

Moderation

Pressure to regulate the exposure of users to content that incites violence and increasingly to content that violates the shifting and evolving definitions of hate speech have generated a variety of platform-specific (and cross-platform) technological moderation strategies. These strategies can be loosely categorised under James Grimmelmann's definition of moderation as "the governance mechanisms that structure participation in a community to facilitate cooperation and prevent abuse" (2015, 42). The breadth of the definition appropriately captures the complexities of operationalising moderation on social media platforms and the resulting impact on the various stakeholders involved – government, industry, security services, and civil society.

Debates on moderation have become increasingly loud, particularly in the policy domain. However, the requirement for some aspects of moderation have long roots in the online environment. As Gillespie writes: "The fantasy of a truly 'open' platform is powerful, resonating with deep, utopian notions of community and democracy – but it is just that, a fantasy. There is no platform that does not impose rules, to some degree. Not to do so would simply be untenable" (2018, 5). The tensions that arise between platforms as marketplaces and as communities, as well as between definitions of private and public spaces, mean that policy formations and practices of moderation are highly contentious. These tensions are especially problematic when content moves into the more nebulous and fluid realms of hate speech (Conway 2020). Participants consistently demonstrated an awareness and concern with the associated issues of privacy and surveillance (Brandtzæg 2012). For instance:

> I mean, I do agree about the regulation thing but then again I just wonder how are they going to cover all of this – like how are they going to cover the regulation – what is allowed, what's not allowed – because nowadays – like for Instagram you can do livestream – like you cannot block something on livestream. So, if it suddenly pops up like the gory image – like all this murder and stuff – It suddenly pops out in a livestream and you can't bock that. So, I think – yeah, I mean, it's – I think it's hard for them to regulate them and set the boundaries.

One of the moderation strategies employed by a variety of platforms such as Facebook, Instagram, and Snapchat is the use of flagging mechanisms. These incorporate platform- specific technological algorithms, user-generated reports, and human moderation. The implementation of flagging varies widely across platforms and the degree of perceived effort involved in the process was noted by participants as influencing the likelihood of their engaging in moderation processes. Platforms such as Instagram were reported as having an easier system that involved "just pressing two buttons," while others were harder to identify, such as on Snapchat, or required considerable investment by users as on Facebook. For some participants the increased effort and associated feed-back from the platform generated a positive sense of affirmation that influenced their future behaviour. One noted: "I feel like Instagram you don't feel as satisfied as if you flagged on Facebook just because Facebook's more in detail." Another that:

> It does take a bit of a while because there's a lot to process and a lot to read but as long as you know that you're getting a reply back and they're putting it down . . . on Instagram, when you see an image and then you come back to it and ooh it's put down because of blah blah blah . . . that's when I feel better, yeah. Then again, it's still out there on the Internet.

While participants were aware of these user-participation moderation strat-egies, many still chose to not report content. Participants described a sense of futility around reporting content because of what was described as an over-whelming amount of materials readily available on the Internet and the likeli-hood it would be reposted or shared elsewhere. As one participant stated: "I'd just see it and then close it. I don't really feel like reporting it is going to do much because it's just going to be uploaded somewhere else."

Decisions not to report also reflected the previously described sense among participants that violent extremist content served an educational purpose, offer-ing insights into what was happening in the rest of the world: "To be fair, even if you do report, just because it's online doesn't mean it's not happening in real life somewhere else. So, what's the point?" Or: "I don't report it . . . but I do try and find more information on it. Maybe is the person still alive, is the victim still alive, are they still okay, were there any repercussions for the perpetrators, that sort of thing."

Social media companies such as Facebook, Instagram, and YouTube have also sought to extend users' sense of agency in viewing content that falls into the grey area of unsuitability by using content warnings. These warnings provide users with a high-level indication that the content is potentially problematic along with a requirement for users to proactively click on the warning to then view the content.

This strategy however arguably taps into curiosity, one of the most frequently cited emotions among participants, as reflected in the statements: "Yeah, I press it. I'm just too curious, I want to see what it is." And: "I get tempted to click and look, just because it's hidden. It's like you're curious. It raises your curiosity . . . . Usually on Instagram it has those warning signs like . . . sensitive . . . . I still click it."

Participants were not necessarily averse to the presence of these warnings recognising that they have the potential to protect an imagined other who does not succumb to or experience their own curiosity. Encounters with this form of online safety advice also need to be considered in the broader context of a user's online experiences and the important role peer-to-peer expectation and pressure can play in consuming this type of content. There is the potential that having heard from peers about content (that now has or already had warnings), the actual encounter is not "negative" for the individual and results in a gradual discrediting of safety advice and standards set by a social media company (Staksrud and Livingstone 2009, 382). Two examples illustrate this point:

> Sometimes curiosity is the driving force for you to see things because you want to know what's happening, but it's a good thing that Facebook has that part that they can cover the bloody part or the picture so that other people don't have to look at it.
>
> Just social media in general, they usually censor – ask – if content's going to be very violent and whatnot, usually young people will just press okay, and straight away the video appears. It's shocking. You know what you're going to see but you still want to see it, I guess. Do you know what I mean?

Although these warning strategies arguably prepare the user for content that is likely to be confronting and disturbing, they may increase an individual's exposure to said content. This reflects the questionability of user-generated moderation strategies that seek to rely on individuals' common sense. As Gillespie notes, "there is something circular about continuing to gesture to common sense of platforms where obscenity and harassment have proven so common" (2018, 51). The close association between warnings and curiosity raises significant questions on the aim and effect of these moderation strategies. Once again this highlights the challenges of formulating strategies without embedding the perspective of a key audience.

The Art of Talking

Communication remains an essential element for countering violent extremism strategies and programs (Davies et al. 2016; Gielen 2019; Koehler 2017; Nasser-Eddine et al. 2011). These strategies are believed to contribute to protective factors against violent extremism: connectedness to society and community; trust and confidence in institutions; and strong social relationships with peers, families, and communities (Urbis 2018). It is not however just the act of talking that is important but how, with whom, and when, dialogue is constructed that makes it effective. The desire to discuss their experiences with online violent extremist content emerged throughout the focus groups: "It's kind of like a conversation starter as well, which is weird, but it's – you definitely do talk about it offline more than online."

However, the people and communities participants were willing or able to talk with about their experiences online highlight the ongoing consequences of high levels of concern among adults, not just about viewing such content but the likely consequences of such engagement (Williams and Kleinman 2014):

> I think because it is so taboo, you can't really go "Mum, I watched this really extremist video and it's affected me in this way." Because obviously you know your parents aren't going to react great to that and your teachers, they're not going to react great to it.

This preference for communication with those perceived as similar, often peer-to-peer, was a consistent finding across all focus groups. Here a shared sense of lived experience was perceived as more likely to result in shared understandings and a more empathetic or sympathetic audience. For example:

Participant 1: Mainly peers . . . basically, yeah, just people who we trust
Participant 2: Mostly peers, like the first people that I would talk to is my peers. I feel like just because you can relate to them more as well.

It provided participants with a means of cathartically managing their emotions, while equally reaffirming social norms around violent extremist content:

> My friend sent it to the chat and we were talking about it. We were like, this is – what an absolute dick and stuff in the chat. What else did we say? I remember having a full conversation about it. My mate's like, this – my mate who showed it to us, he was like look at this. This is the most horrible thing I've ever seen . . . yeah and then we all had a conversation about it, how messed up. How fucked up what just happened was. Yeah. We were just talking – we didn't really talk – go into much detail.

The last sentence of the above quote is indicative of the superficial nature ascribed to these peer-to-peer discussions by most participants. Despite the perceived trust and connection to the audience, the resulting conversations were described as largely shallow and impacted by peer pressures that link back to previous discussions around bragging rights and perceived social conventions on the "correct" emotions to express:

When – for me – when she opened the Snapchat with me – my friend, it was quite superficial. She was just like, Aha! He does this all the time. I mean for me, I was quite shocked [laughs].

Yep, just shallow. Yeah, very shallow conversation, yeah. Yeah, we don't – because we show no consideration in those conversations to the people – the victims in the video. We're always just like, did you see that video? Yeah, it's gross, hey? We just carry on doing work.

Several participants described how the size of the group affected both the expression of emotions and the depth of discussion. For example:

Participant 1: It's usually superficial
Participant 2: Yeah, but it depends, because if you're in a big group, and the person who first reacts – the person who reacts to it first, is usually how everyone reacts to as well

Another noted that:

It just really depends on how big the group is. If it's like a one-on-one, I feel like it's more – you can go deeper in to talk about it. Whereas in groups, it really depends on how everyone reacts to it. Everyone just follows.

While it is not the intention here to question the centrality of dialogue within the broader scholarship on countering violent extremism, these findings reiterate the importance of drawing on the experience of young people in the formation of policy and procedure (Gibson and Trnka 2020). What does effective, resilient, focused communication on violent extremist content look and feel like for young people? Are there any potential benefits of these superficial conversations? How can these conversations be drawn upon and extended to facilitate the generation of resilient curative strategies for young people? Most participants were unable to articulate what this would look like or how this could be achieved.

When young people communicate on, in, and with digital contexts, they navigate norms and expectations about what it means to participate in each relationship, group, or community. Social media also provides a venue for offering real-time peer affirmation; this is demonstrated through liking, commenting on, and sharing posts. However, as the above quotes demonstrate, opportunities to connect with trusted audiences such as peers and friends is arguably a double-edged sword. On one level it facilitates closeness and connectivity to community through shared experiences and emotions, while on the other it generates pressure to maintain and perform certain emotions and behaviours (James et al. 2017). At times, participants expressed a sense of discombobulation, an unease and uncomfortableness about the simultaneous emotions and behaviours they engaged in as they curated their way through the online environment. They were left unsure about how they should react and noted that they felt a lack of guidance or insight as to the appropriate ways to navigate through these encounters. For example:

> But that [video I watched] was a shock video and you're told to be shocked. It's like here, watch this, it's all pop culture in a way sometimes, you're told to be shocked at this but they don't tell you what to do after you've seen the video, other than that's disgusting. You're not really told what to do if you're really traumatised by it.

And:

> Just I always feel like disgusting. I think why I'm doing like such a happy life – I mean when I see the animals being abused, I reflect on myself and reflect on my whole life. I don't know what this kind of feeling is called.

These statements suggest a possibility for raising young people's emotional intelligence as part of effective communication strategies.

However, if we conceptualising resilience as a process of learning to deal with problematic issues, it also highlights the important role held by real-world engagement with complex and difficult materials in generating resilience, particularly given the impossibility and appropriateness of restricting exposure completely to online violent extremist content (Vandoninck, d'Haenens, and Roe 2013). It also raises a question as to the potential utility this sense of unease and disquiet may offer to those seeking to increase the protective strategies available to young people as they resiliently navigate their online and offline environments.

5 Radicalisation to Violent Extremism

Does the Internet create terrorists? No other question so dominates research into how and why terrorists use the Internet, and whether individuals potentially become radicalised to perform violence through exposure to online violent extremist content. This question also influences public debate, at times bordering on hysteria, among media, politicians, and concerned parents about the risks presented by young people's exposure to violent and extreme online material (Aly et al. 2017). Over the past decade these fears have been stoked by the actions of terrorists themselves. Most notable has been the flood of sophisticated online communications and propaganda produced by the self-styled Islamic State, contributing to thousands of people from across the globe leaving their homes to join IS's supposed caliphate (Bergin et al. 2015). There have also been very deliberate attempts by far-right shooters to weaponize social media to spread their message and violent tactics as widely as possible (Thomas 2020). As a result, a societal fear has emerged that unsupervised access to online extremist content can remotely control young people into joining terrorist movements or becoming "lone wolves," radicalised – even brainwashed – individuals who suddenly turn on society due to a mysterious process of online radicalisation.

This section explores what young people, who are immersed in a digital environment containing terrorist and violent extremist content, actually think about the concept of radicalisation. It discusses their own fears about their and their friends' exposure to this material, and also examines just how conscious young people are of the reasons why terrorists and violent extremists produce this material with the intention that it will go viral.

The evidence for any simple slide into violent extremism – due solely to access to violent extremist online clips, memes, and other forms of propaganda – reveals a complicated relationship between the Internet and radicalisation to terrorism (Ferguson 2016; Neumann 2013). For example, in a cross-sectional examination of jihadist information-seeking and cognitive radicalisation, Frissen (2021) demonstrates how young people seeking out jihadist beheading videos were more likely motivated by curiosity than by a precursor to radical-isation. This followed the mainstreaming of these videos through traditional media dissemination and their incorporation in popular culture. These nuances are further supported in broader literature that has shown how the concept of the self-starting, digitally-enabled "lone wolf" terrorist is a gross oversimplification (Schuurman et al. 2019; Von Behr, I., Reding, A., Edwards, C. and Gribbon, L. 2013). Yet, in our focus groups it was clear that widespread public and political concern about the online radicalisation of youth has shaped young people's own attitudes and perceptions about their relationship to digital media. For instance, in response to public debates about terrorism on the Internet, the concept of online radicalisation has been examined in high school classes, with one female stating that "in Year 11 and 12 ... we looked at extremism and massacres ... in-depth and why people would do this and how people get radicalised through videos like this." This was part of an optional Society and Culture curriculum and, although the participant recalled their teacher as being inspirational, students were also left with a sense of anxiety about their online habits and exposure. Will I, perhaps, become a terrorist if I expose myself to unfiltered social media streams?

A number of participants expressed anxiety that either they, or more com-monly their more "vulnerable" friends, could be influenced by online violent extremist content. This observation is concurrent with research into strongly evidenced phenomena of third-person effects, where individuals overestimate the influence media has on others in comparison with themselves (Eisend 2017). It was assumed that exposure to violent and extreme online content could affect different people in different ways and, even, "I don't know, someone in this room" may be vulnerable. As one participant put it:

> [T]here's that stereotype about the quiet kid being the one that's going to end up shooting the school or whatever. But it is concerning that anyone in this room could somehow become radicalised and turn into a – you know. But I think you've got to be careful about who you share your content to and all that. That's why I only share with my really close friends.

Third-person effect has often been explained through the presence of a self-serving bias whereby people think they are more likely to have the requisite knowledge, expertise, and resilience to engage with the communications than are others. The impact of the third-person effect on the generation of an individual's resilience is an area that would benefit from increased research, particularly in relation to the behavioural impacts associated with fact-checking and with the motivations of content producers (Corbu et al. 2020).

Yet instead of a fear of becoming radicalised, young people were more often – and perhaps with more justification – worried that they would be perceived by parents or teachers as at risk of radicalisation if they discussed their viewing habits or any concerns they had about the content they consumed. Participants raised this anxiety on many occasions, sometimes breaking out into conversations among themselves without any prompting or input from facilitators:

Participant 1: I wouldn't talk to adults about it [online violent extremist content], because I'd felt like they would just exaggerate the situation. Even though it is pretty serious, I feel like they would even take it up to 11.
Participant 2: Do you think that they would accuse you of being radicalised?
Participant: Yeah, exactly.
Multiple Participants: Yeah.
Participant 1: They'll take away your computer.

This fear of being seen as someone who could potentially become radicalised to terrorism has created a chilling effect on young people's willingness to communicate with adults about their online experiences. A not-unjustified fear of being labelled a terrorist, or on a slippery slope to becoming a terrorist, may well be deleterious to their mental health and ability to navigate these online spaces. This fear presents its own risks that are quite distinct from any actual processes of online radicalisation to terrorism. We observed this to be especially the case for young people from non-Anglo-Saxon backgrounds (particularly the Middle East) or who are Islamic. As one such participant observed: "If you tell someone, it's not going to be them going, okay, well let's talk about this. It's going to be followed by 1,000 questions asking, How did you find it? Why are you watching this? It's not followed with help; it's followed with more questions."

Despite these concerns, as has been shown throughout this research, young people are not simply passive content consumers of content, vulnerable to being remotely manipulated and radicalised to violence online by scheming terrorists. Instead, young people consistently presented us with a wide range of responses to concerns about the effects that violent extremist online material were having on them and their friends. They also demonstrated a robust ability to interact with difficult material in ways that, while necessarily exploratory and messy, do perhaps demonstrate a form of resilience-building. This is an insight into young people's relationship with difficult online spaces that is not often presented in research or in public debate on the dangers of radicalisation. However, it should be taken into consideration when the risks of online exposure to violent and extreme content are discussed.

Radicalisation

It's not "as simple as someone seeing a video." This sentiment was repeatedly expressed by young people when discussing hypothetical online radicalisation. Participants noted at many points that they could not relate to the type of thinking that would lead people to respond to violent online content with a desire to emulate that violence, to "join a war," or "become a terrorist."

> Yeah, and so in real life with our generation that's never really occurred, not to my knowledge and I don't think anyone who's ever seen sort of like Islamic extremism violence has ever thought, Ooh I want to go do that. It's just such a bizarre sort of thought to think.

Young people were also quick to relate the concept of radicalisation back to familiar debates about the supposed violent and dangerous nature of video gaming. In these cases, they adamantly rejected any clear or simple causation between either violent video games or violent extremist content online and the adoption of violence in the "real world."

> I'm not going to play Call of Duty and then want to run around and do all this crazy stuff. So, I wouldn't watch a video of street gangs in a Mexican cartel and go, Ooh I want to be a street gangster in the cartel in Mexico. I feel like that's definitely not a sort of relation to be honest.

While these perspectives may reveal a naiveté about demonstrated examples where exposure to online violent extremist content has enabled and facilitated a radicalisation process; for examples, see Neumann (2013). They also reinforce the emerging academic consensus that cases of online self-radicalisation are extremely rare (Von Behr et al.2013), and that in almost all cases exposure to digital content is only one factor in a complicated multi-factored process (Scrivens, Gill, and Conway 2020; Meleagrou-Hitchens, Alexander, and Kaderbhai 2017; Frissen 2021).

Yet, a tendency to look for simplistic and politically palatable answers to the problem of terrorism has a long history in academia and has influenced public debates on the topic. Immediately after the al-Qaeda terrorist attacks in the United States on September 11, 2001, Western researchers became highly incentivized to find solutions to the problems of terrorism, who becomes a terrorist, and why (Sageman 2014). This led initially to the presentation of a series of monocausal explanations, including economic deprivation (Krieger and Meierrieks 2011), foreign conflicts (Pape 2003), social bonds (Sageman 2008), and a quest for significance and meaning (Kruglanski et al. 2014). While diverse, these attempts to answer the problem of terrorism were all similar in that they were overly simplistic and, at first, did not consider that an online dimension played any crucially significant role. The July 7, 2005, bombings in London, carried out by English-born nationals inspired by al-Qaeda propaganda at home began a shift in thinking about the online dimensions of terrorist recruitment (Kirby 2007) – a shift that was accelerated by the subsequent creation of extensive online media strategies by al-Qaeda and, later, by Islamic State (Weimann and Hoffman 2015; Droogan and Peattie 2017; Droogan and Peattie 2018). Soon, scholars were considering exposure to online violent and extreme content as central to the process of becoming a terrorist (Stenersen 2008), and "online radicalisation" joined the ranks of monocausal explanations simplistically addressing the problem of terrorism. This radicalisation thesis reached its most extreme formulation in the discredited idea of the "lone wolf," an individual who becomes radicalised to terrorist action purely online and in isolation from any other people and factors (Post, McGinnis, and Moody 2014). It's a concept that unfortunately came to influence much media and public hand-wringing about the dangers posed by the Internet for the vulnerable young (Burke 2017).

In a context where both the terrorist threat and the academic and practitioner understanding of that threat were fluid and fast-changing, it was not long before exposure to online extremist materials, in particular the brutal and voyeuristic content produced by al-Qaeda and Islamic State and shared widely on message boards and social media, was considered enough to reinforce or even create violent extremism in those unlucky enough to encounter it. The Internet and social media became the new battleground between terrorists and government-employed counter-terrorism practitioners (Weimann and Hoffman 2015), with the minds of young people as the pawns.

This assumption about the vulnerability of young people to online radicalisation, and a simplistic understanding of the way in which media affects consumers, never addressed the overwhelming fact that while many, or even most, young people have experienced some form of terrorist propaganda online, remarkably few have shown any signs of becoming radicalised. Indeed, the wider complexity of the situation, particularly the diverse ways in which young people consume this material, was well expressed by one of our participants when they discussed watching Islamic State beheading videos:

> I think those videos were more geared towards a different audience. They don't make this just so a teenager can laugh at it, or watch it, and change their world views. They use it to – they make it for a different reason than why I watched it. I wasn't there to learn about what they want me to become. I watched it because I just wanted to see what they do. But I think it differs from the producers.

Participants in focus groups were adamant that exposure to online violent and extreme content does not "brainwash" or "hypnotize" you." That does not mean, however, that they saw exposure to this content as unproblematic. Indeed, there was a common sentiment expressed that it could adversely affect "a very small percentage" of their peers. One participant responded to this debate by stating that rather than "just hypnotize" us, a more complex process occurs among her friends where some young people may be channelled towards more dangerous places through "emotion[s] like sympathy or anger to give them purpose." These comments chime with both the theme of this volume as well as the emerging academic consensus around the more limited dangers of the Internet for terrorist radicalisation (Waldek, Ballsun-Stanton, and Droogan 2020). As Alastair Reed (2018), writing for the International Centre for Counter-terrorism at The Hague, put it:

> One of the enduring myths about "online" violent extremist propaganda is the extent to which it plays a direct role in radicalisation. If we were to believe the reporting in many newspapers, we would have the impression that online propaganda has the ability to radicalize individuals by itself, posing a new and direct threat potentially radicalizing the nation's youth directly on their computers.

Instead, research shows that most people who come into contact with online extremist content are not radicalised, and, indeed, that the vast majority of those who do decide to pursue violent extremism are exposed to extremist ideology offline, usually through social networks and live person-to-person contacts (Ferguson 2016; Brown and Cowls 2015; Frissen 2021). This relates to Conway's (2017) powerful argument that the Internet itself does not cause radicalisation because exposure does not lead to violence in the vast majority of cases; most engagement with violent and extreme content (such as sharing or liking) is mere "clicktivism," and face-to-face interaction is regularly shown to be far more successful in radicalising individuals to adopt extremism and violence.

Digital media is increasingly understood as more of a catalyst or facilitator, rather than as a simple gateway. The Internet and social media certainly provide a host of previously unavailable opportunities for terrorists and violent extremists to promote, advertise, and recruit (Droogan and Waldek 2019), but these opportunities affect different people in radically different ways, with the Internet providing pathways into violence for some, but only in combination with a range of other personal and social factors (Gill et al. 2017; Scrivens, Gill, and Conway 2020). Young people we interviewed were usually aware of media stories of people who had supposedly been radicalised online, but understood that cases such as these were rare, and that factors other than simple exposure to violent and extreme content were involved. As one male respondent phrased it:

> I feel like it does though for some people. Like every few months on the news you'll hear of some story of some like eighteen-to-21-year-old who's trying to fly out of the country to go to the Middle East to join ISIS and they've just been stopped at the airport. So, I feel like for a very small percentage it does actually get to them.

The concept of vulnerability came up regularly in discussions, with participants suggesting that some young people who experience bullying, domestic violence, or other forms of harm and social disconnection, may be more likely to use violent and extreme material accessed on the Internet as an outlet. Those without "common sense" or who didn't feel "sympathy," or felt it for the wrong people, were seen as being particularly vulnerable. In addition, significant trauma and bullying were factors mentioned by a number of respondents. However, there was a sentiment that this would need to be more than just "being bullied on Fortnite [and then] go around and shoot people."

> Yeah. I feel like you have to be vulnerable in order for that stuff to get to you. Like say if someone was being bullied at school and they don't have a good home life, then the only way they can seek refuge out of that would be maybe through these videos. Because they're exposed to these videos and these videos helped them in that time of need, they would sort of sympathise as you said with these foreigners and be like, Ooh okay, yeah I'd rather join them and feel like I'm part of a group rather than stay here and be disconnected from their family

In addition to emotional or psychological vulnerabilities such as bullying or victimization, two external factors were repeatedly raised as contributing to potential radicalisation: the geographical location of the user and the volume of extremist content presented on their social media feeds.

The concern young people expressed about violent extremism increased when the event or content was closer to their own lives and homes. Their perceptions of who may or may not be affected by the content was impacted by distance and geographical context. Conflict zones such as "the Middle East" or "places like America where school shootings occur" were seen as producing particular vulnerabilities. For instance, there was a perception among some focus group participants that school shootings in the United States, such as the 1999 Columbine massacre, were "fuelled from violent extremist videos." The danger here, it was argued, stemmed from a combination of mainstream and social media reporting of these events, and the thrills and notoriety this could bestow upon the perpetrators in their narcissistic quest for infamy. Because "they get so much media attention and they get so much – they become immortalised as whatever – like they still get spoken about – they have a song 'Pumped Up Kicks' about it." Mainstream media was seen as playing a key role (as opposed to just social media) because, as with the song, it "can definitely plant a seed in someone's head and go oh look what happened there. They're still talked about today." The assumption seems to be that it is the mainstream media's saturation reporting of school shootings that creates a media environment that is attractive to some individuals craving the "kick" of instant and ongoing fame through the perpetration of horrific violence. Ironically, mainstream media's reporting on the radicalisation of young people via online exposure likewise draws attention to the existence of violent extremist material, rendering it "taboo" and potentially appealing for some to seek out.

The geographical distance involved was likely another factor in the perception that school shootings may be more related to media exposure than, say, violent extremism or video gaming. A repeated theme during discussion was that the closer to home an event occurred, the more concerning it was and the more real the threat of radicalisation became. As one participant from a placid Sydney suburb put it:

> There was also that [Sydney] Epping Boys thing, where a few Epping Boys students a few years ago tried to leave for Syria but they got caught ... so it was knowing that someone in a school near mine could become radicalised is concerning.

Participants argued that, in addition to geography, the scale and volume of exposure to online violent extremist material may play a role in determining why some of their supposedly more vulnerable peers potentially become radicalised to violence. One male participant argued that extremist groups that "have a massive social media presence" and "stream a lot of stuff" could lead to a situation where people "dive straight in" and end up leaving "the country and try to do all this crazy stuff." Another suggested that "if they see it on a daily basis, or it's always on your suggested page under things, it will affect their mind-set and how they think."

Despite this concern about repeated and prolonged exposure, there was a marked naivety among young people about the specific ways in which social media platforms funnel content towards users based upon their users' previous browsing history, and the subsequent creation of algorithm-enabled "echo chambers" or filter bubbles (Schlegel 2019). Certainly, there is substantial evidence that the Internet can strengthen people's ideological convictions through repeated exposure to a single perspective. Research on areas as diverse as political polarization, the creation of communities centred on conspiracy theories, and terrorism recruitment illustrate how this process of "echo-chamber" creation can lead to the isolation and gradual immersion in the communities that inhabit these cut-off online spaces (Baumann et al. 2020; Lima et al. 2018; O'Hara and Stevens 2015). However, no participants reflected on this process during discussions of their online behaviour.

Understanding Why Terrorists Do What They Do

During each focus group, participants were asked the questions "Why do you think people produce violent and extremist materials?" "Why do they post them online or share them?" and "How do they want you to react?" These questions go to the heart of the issue of why and how terrorists and violent extremists harness the potential affordances offered by the Internet and digital media. However, they also address the much larger issues of why terrorists consider the media to be important in the first place, why terrorist violence is so often performed as a type of public spectacle, and the importance of having an audience for this violence is in the success of terrorist strategies. These issues pre-date the adoption of the Internet and digital media by modern groups like Islamic State or far-right extremists. Indeed, they stretch back well before the invention of computers to the dawn of modern terrorism in the European anarchist movements of the late nineteenth century (Rapoport 2001). They are central to understanding the very nature of terrorism as a strategy of communication intent on the violent coercion of public sentiment.

Most definitions of terrorism include a clause that indicates that terrorist violence, or threats of violence, are performed essentially to coerce an audience (Schmid 2013). This is done primarily through the cultivation and wide dissemination of the raw emotions of fear and terror among the public.

Whether the intended audience is the general public or a political elite, it is acknowledged that the media plays a crucial role in broadcasting propaganda of the violent deed, rather than of the mere word. Seen from the perspective of its intent, terrorist violence is an atrocious but essentially pragmatic hook used to captivate public attention and engineer a desired societal reaction – be it recruitment, capitulation, or revolution. In this way, terrorism can basically be understood as a form of communication, – a strategy of coercing people to do what terrorists wish, and one in which the media, digital or otherwise, plays an essential role (Nacos 2016). As the historian of terrorism Walter Laqueur (2001) stated, "A terrorist strike without media coverage defeats the purpose of the exercise." Or, in the words of Brian Jenkins (1974), "terrorism is theatre" and they "want a lot of people watching, not a lot of people dead."

Despite the widespread and dramatic impact of terrorism and counter-terrorism on Western society over more than twenty years since September 11, 2001, the general public still poorly understands the basic media communication strategy used by terrorists to effect change (Vergani 2018). Young people we spoke to who, in most cases, had grown up entirely within the post–9/11 world, were often at a loss to explain why violent extremist propaganda was disseminated online. Answers to this question included "they take joy in it," "something [was] wrong with their upbringing," they "had nothing else better to do," or that they are purely "disturbed," "mentally unstable," or "evil doers." Other respondents suggested a religious motivation because of their "undying love for Allah," or that they "want to be remembered," or they did it solely for "money." A few respondents got closer to touching on the media communications strategy of terrorists stating that they create and post violent materials to inform the world about taboo topics and "what really happens," or for "shock value," or perhaps "to get more likes or becoming the next big influencer."

One popular response to this question of motivation acknowledged the fundamental attention-seeking nature of online violent and extreme content but did not connect this with any understanding of its wider strategic purpose (i.e., to influence and coerce an audience through fear). According to this perspective, violent online content was produced and posted to "get attention" or as "an instrument for people who wanted to gain notoriety." These answers were almost always given in connection with the livestreamed 2019 Christchurch mosque attacks. It was noted that the perpetrator engaged in classic online attention-seeking strategies: referencing popular memes such as the YouTuber PewDiePie, using music, and engaging with the audience prior to the shooting (Thomas, 2020).

However, even in this case, young people mostly answered the question of the perpetrator's motivation in carrying out the attack and broadcasting it online as if it were a simple desire for attention. As one male respondent suggested, the attack was produced so "you'd watch a video and you'd go, there's no point to this [video] besides showing violent content. I mean it's attention." There was no acknowledgement that the attacker used digital media in order to either promote a cause or to elicit a response from the viewing audience. The attack was considered random, evil, attention-seeking behaviour devoid of any wider or more sinister ideological purpose.

This simplistic understanding of the basic motivation for the creation and dissemination of violent extremist material online reveals that young people, while sophisticated in their navigation of these online spaces, are for the most part fundamentally naive about the wider reasons for their existence. When asked "how do you think these content creators want you to react to the material" participants put forward "anger," "raise hate," and "instil fear," but were unsure why these responses would be desirable. There was little or no awareness of the concept of narrowcasting: that online platforms can be used by violent extremists to reach expanded audiences, or to engage and target specific demographics, such as youth, through tailored messaging (Weimann and Hoffman 2015). In only one discussion about Islamic State and al-Qaeda materials were the terms "brand awareness," "marketing tool," or "recruitment" raised.

Among the sample, a single participant did present a more sophisticated understanding of the strategy employed by the Christchurch perpetrator. According to this participant, the shooter aimed to "get his message out there to as many people as possible" in order to garner sympathy and "inspire them to do something similar." His strategy was deemed to have been successful because his anti-immigration ideas, presented in a self-penned manifesto uploaded prior to the attack, were discussed in the mainstream media and sparked a wider public debate. He was able to get his message across and we will "always remember that this person did it."

While we don't expect young people to be sophisticated experts on terrorism, this finding coupled with the emotion of curiosity previously discussed presents an opportunity for programs that increase resilience through education about strategies of violence.

6 Conclusion

This Element began with the horrors of the Christchurch terrorist attack in New Zealand. The perpetrator's strategic use of a confluence of technology and appropriation of popular online culture ensured the content went viral. In doing so, the attack and the digital content it generated spoke directly to the widespread societal concern associated with online youth radicalisation to violent extremism. This is a concern, even panic, that has been reinforced by the Covid-19 pandemic, increasing the time young people spend online and consequently their likely exposure to violent extremist content. It has never been our intention to question the risks that arise from the relationship between digital media and violent extremism. As Berger notes: "Social media provided [extremists with] an inexpensive platform to reach massive audiences, emphasizing virality and controversy over social norms" (2018, 148). Yet questions remain as to why, given the prevalence of such content and the presumed vulnerability of young people, only a very small number of those exposed to this type of content ever go on to engage in violent extremism. We have sought to challenge and problematise the underpinning ideas that have contributed to a widespread societal concern that has been a defining feature of our time – the assumption of a passive and vulnerable audience and the effectiveness of and role played by violent extremist content on processes of radicalisation. We are cognizant of the limitations of the data we collected. However, in giving voice to the young people at the heart of these concerns, a fascinating snapshot emerges of the diverse and dynamic emotional and behavioural strategies young people draw upon to curate the often violent and extreme digital environment.

Although we draw on a formal academic definition of violent extremism, it should be noted that participants' understanding of this type of content was at times wide-reaching, incorporating videos depicting gore, gang violence, suicide, violence against animals and human foetuses, among others. All of this points to a digital environment littered with many types of violent extremism that are impossible to fully ignore. Yet as the numerous quotes from participants detail, young people are able to circumnavigate this environment in ways that at times are both concerning and surprising. We cannot assume that the objectives of the producers of violent extremism that includes the cultivation of emotions such as terror, fear, anger, and perhaps hope or redemption, are uniformly experienced and reproduced by young people. This is not a passive one-way relationship. Instead, the participants repeatedly caveated their initial expressions of shock, horror, and fear, with a discussion of other emotions such as curiosity and humour. These emotions were also not experienced in the singular but rather participants spoke to a far more nuanced and complex response that simultaneously incorporated positive and negative emotions.

These emotions were expressed and experienced within an environment defined by its sociality. Our findings reiterated that the key role social relationships have on the experiences of young people and the digital environment is one defined by sociality. Young people's experiences and behaviours were shaped by, and in turn were shaping, the social relationships they had with their peers, family members, educators, and broader adult populations online and offline. However, to solely define this sociality through a lens of risk, danger, and concern is to miss the bigger picture. Even where participants discussed violent extremist content as a source of humour, as a means of bragging rights, or as a means of better understanding the world, there was a shared sense that the content remained in some way morally distasteful or wrong. Social relationships can be problematic, but equally they can reaffirm normative attitudes to violent extremism and in doing so provide potential opportunities to strengthen the resilience of young people.

From this confluence of emotions, sociality, and technology, there emerged a broad spectrum of behavioural responses. It became increasingly apparent that warning-based moderation strategies employed by many social media companies were not just ineffective but arguably increased the likelihood users would engage with the dangerous or risky content. This suggests that while there has been an absence of emotion-centric research within terrorism studies, the same can be said for social media companies. The importance of emotion in understanding behavioural responses to violent extremist content was further reiterated in the discussions held around moderation. Although many participants seemed to be in favour of some form of control over the exposure to violent extremist content, this was often discussed as a requirement for others, as opposed to themselves. This reluctance and even at times aversion to moderation in part reflects the strong presence of curiosity among the participants. Rather than radicalising these individuals towards violent extremism, participants expressed a desire to learn more about those involved or specific events both for purposes of general education and to learn more about the world. As one participant noted: "it helps us to make our world a much smaller place." These findings add another layer of complexity to the debates around online moderation.

In capturing and articulating the experiences of young people, we have identified a series of opportunities that may exist to build upon and develop their resilience to the possible risks associated with repeated exposure to violent extremist content. It became increasingly clear that despite their experience of such content and the sophisticated strategies they described in response to such content, their understanding of the phenomenon of violent extremism – including the reasons why such content may have been created – was naive. This was particularly interesting given the emergence of curiosity as a dominant emotion among participants. Young people expressed a desire to know more about the content and violent extremism, and they described strategies to address this curiosity; however they continually found themselves engaged in relatively shallow and superficial discussions. We note an absence of investigations that examine the benefit of deep versus shallow discussions as a means of fostering resilience to violent extremism. However, recognising the emotion of curiosity and the absence of knowledge about strategies of violence represents a tangible opportunity to increase resilience.

This research aimed to problematise the idea that young people represented a vulnerable audience open to infection by violent extremist content. In presenting the voices of young people we argue that it is necessary to reach out to these audiences and understand their lived emotional and behavioural experiences of violent extremist content. Only in this way can we can hope to better develop effective moderation and resilience-building strategies that allow young people to navigate through an environment from which violent extremist content is unlikely to ever fully disappear.

References

Ahmed, Sara. 2014. *Cultural Politics of Emotion*. Edinburgh: Edinburgh University Press.

Ahn, Dohyun, and Dong-Hee Shin. 2013. "Is the Social Use of Media for Seeking Connectedness or for Avoiding Social Isolation? Mechanisms Underlying Media Use and Subjective Well-Being." *Computers in Human Behavior* 29 (6): 2453–62.

Al-Rawi, Ahmed. 2016. "Anti-ISIS Humor: Cultural Resistance of Radical Ideology." *Politics, Religion & Ideology* 17 (1): 52–68.

Altheide, David L. 2006. "Terrorism and the Politics of Fear." *Cultural Studies ↔ Critical Methodologies* 6 (4): 415–39.

Aly, Anne. 2017. "Brothers, Believers, Brave Mujahideen: Focusing Attention on the Audience of Violent Jihadist Preachers." *Studies in Conflict and Terrorism* 40 (1): 62–76.

Aly, Anne, Stuart Macdonald, Lee Jarvis, and Thomas M. Chen. 2017. "Introduction to the Special Issue: Terrorist Online Propaganda and Radicalization." *Studies in Conflict and Terrorism* 40 (1): 1–9.Anderson, Monica, and Jingjing Jiang. 2018. "Teens, Social Media & Technology 2018." Pew Research Center. May 31, 2018. www.pewresearch.org/internet/2018/05/31/teens-social-media-technology-2018/.

Atran, Scott. 2011a. "Who Becomes a Terrorist Today?" In *The Ethics and Efficacy of the Global War on Terrorism: Fighting Terror with Terror*, edited by Charles P. Webel and John A. Arnaldi, 45–58. New York: Palgrave Macmillan US.

2011b. *Talking to the Enemy: Religion, Brotherhood, and the (Un)Making of Terrorists*. Reprint edition. Scranton, PA: Ecco.

2015. "Why ISIS Has the Potential to Be a World-Altering Revolution." Aeon. December 15, 2015. https://aeon.co/essays/why-isis-has-the-potential-to-be-a-world-altering-revolution.

Baumann, Fabian, Philipp Lorenz-Spreen, Igor M. Sokolov, and Michele Starnini. 2020. "Modeling Echo Chambers and Polarization Dynamics in Social Networks." *Physical Review Letters* 124 (4): 048301.

Berger, J. M. 2018. *Extremism*. Essential Knowledge Series. Cambridge, MA: The MIT Press.

Berger, Jonah, and Katherine L. Milkman. 2012. "What Makes Online Content Viral?" *Journal of Marketing Research* 49 (2): 192–205.

Bergin, Anthony, Michael Clifford, David Connery, Peter Jennings, David Lang, Amelia Long, Clare Murphy, Simone Roworth, Rosalyn Turner, and Samina Yasmeen et al. 2015. "Gen Y Jihadists: Preventing Radicalisation in Australia." www.aspi.org.au/report/gen-y-jihadists-pre venting-radicalisation-australia.

Bogle, Ariel. 2019. "Social Media Deserves Blame for Spreading the Christchurch Video, but so Do We." *ABC News*, March 18, 2019. www .abc.net.au/news/science/2019-03-19/facebook-to-blame-for-christ church-live-video-but-so-are-we/10911238.

boyd, danah. 2015. *It's Complicated: The Social Lives of Networked Teens*. New Haven, CT: Yale University Press.

boyd, danah. , and Nicole B. Ellison. 2007. "Social Network Sites: Definition, History, and Scholarship." *Journal of Computer-Mediated Communication: JCMC* 13 (1): 210–30.

Brandtzæg, P. B. 2012. "Social Networking Sites: Their Users and Social implications – A Longitudinal Study." *Journal of Computer-Mediated Communication* 17 (4): 467–88. https://academic.oup.com/jcmc/article-abstract/17/4/467/4067681.

Brewin, C. R. 1996. "Theoretical Foundations of Cognitive-Behavior Therapy for Anxiety and Depression." *Annual Review of Psychology* 47: 33–57.

Brown, Ian, and Josh Cowls. 2015. "Check the Web: Assessing the Ethics and Politics of Policing the Internet for Extremist Material." In *VOX-Pol*. https://doi.org/APO-58979.

Bruns, Axel. 2007. "Produsage: Towards a Broader Framework for User-Led Content Creation." In *Proceedings of 6th ACM SIGCHI Conference on Creativity and Cognition 2007*, edited by Ben Shneiderman, 99–105. Washington, DC: Association for Computing Machinery.

Burke, Jason. 2015. *The New Threat: The Past, Present, and Future of Islamic Militancy*. New York: The New Press.

2017. "The Myth of the 'Lone Wolf' Terrorist." *The Guardian*, March 30, 2017. www.theguardian.com/news/2017/mar/30/myth-lone-wolf-terrorist.

Cantor, Joanne. 1998. "Children's Attraction to Violent Television Programming." In *Why We Watch: The Attractions of Violent Entertainment*, New York: Oxford University Press, 88–115.

Carnagey, Nicholas L., Craig A. Anderson, and Bruce D. Bartholow. 2007. "Media Violence and Social Neuroscience: New Questions and New Opportunities." *Current Directions in Psychological Science* 16 (4): 178–82.

Carver, Charles S., Michael F. Scheier, and Jagdish K. Weintraub. 1989. "Assessing Coping Strategies: A Theoretically Based Approach." *Journal of Personality and Social Psychology* 56 (2): 267–83.

Christchurch Call. n.d. Accessed February 26, 2021. www.christchurchcall.com /call.html.

Conway, Maura. 2017. "Determining the Role of the Internet in Violent Extremism and Terrorism: Six Suggestions for Progressing Research." *Studies in Conflict and Terrorism* 40 (1): 77–98.

———. 2020. "Routing the Extreme Right." *The RUSI Journal* 165 (1): 108–13.

Corbu, Nicoleta, Denisa-Adriana Oprea, Elena Negrea-Busuioc, and Loredana Radu. 2020. "'They Can't Fool Me, but They Can Fool the Others!' Third Person Effect and Fake News Detection." *European Journal of Disorders of Communication: The Journal of the College of Speech and Language Therapists, London* 35 (2): 165–80.

Cottee, Simon. 2015. "Jihadi Cool: Why ISIS Propaganda Is So Powerful." *The Atlantic*, December 24, 2015. www.theatlantic.com/international/archive/ 2015/12/isis-jihadi-cool/421776/.

Cottee, Simon, and Keith Hayward. 2011. "Terrorist (E)motives: The Existential Attractions of Terrorism." *Studies in Conflict and Terrorism* 34 (12): 963–86.

Crawford, Neta C. 2000. "The Passion of World Politics: Propositions on Emotion and Emotional Relationships." *International Security* 24 (4): 116–56.

———. 2013. "Emotions and International Security: Cave! Hic Libido." *Critical Studies on Security* 1 (1): 121–3.

Davies, Garth, Christine Neudecker, Marie Ouellet, Martin Bouchard, and Benjamin Ducol. 2016. "Toward a Framework Understanding of Online Programs for Countering Violent Extremism." *Journal for Deradicalization* 0 (6): 51–86.

DeLisi, Matt, Michael G. Vaughn, Douglas A. Gentile, Craig A. Anderson, and Jeffrey J. Shook. 2013. "Violent Video Games, Delinquency, and Youth Violence: New Evidence." *Youth Violence and Juvenile Justice* 11 (2): 132–42.

Dickson, EJ. 2019. "Why Did the Christchurch Shooter Name-Drop YouTube Phenom PewDiePie?" *Rolling Stone.* 2019. www.rollingstone.com/cul ture/culture-news/pewdie-pie-new-zealand-mosque-shooting-youtube -808633/.

Droogan, Julian, and Shane Peattie. 2017. "Mapping the Thematic Landscape of Dabiq Magazine." *Australian Journal of International Affairs* 71 (6): 591–620.

———. 2018. "Reading Jihad: Mapping the Shifting Themes of Inspire Magazine." *Terrorism and Political Violence* 30 (4): 684–717.

Droogan, Julian, and Lise Waldek. 2019. "Social Media and Terrorism in the Asia Pacific." In *Terrorism and Insurgency in Asia: A Contemporary*

Examination of Terrorist and Separatist Movements, edited by Ben Schreer and Andrew Tan. New York: Routledge, 31–44.

Droogan, Julian, and Shane Peattie. 2017. "Mapping the Thematic Landscape of Dabiq Magazine." *Australian Journal of International Affairs* 71 (6): 591–620.

2018. "Reading Jihad: Mapping the Shifting Themes of Inspire Magazine." *Terrorism and Political Violence* 30 (4): 684–717.

Eder, Jens. 2018. "Collateral Emotions: Political Web Videos and Divergent Audience Responses." In *Cognitive Theory and Documentary Film*, edited by Catalin Brylla and Mette Kramer, 183–203. Cham, Switzerland: Springer International Publishing.

Eisend, Martin. 2017. "The Third-Person Effect in Advertising: A Meta-Analysis." *Journal of Advertising* 46 (3): 377–94.

Elzain, Carol. 2008. "Modern Islamic Terrorism, Jihad and the Perceptions of Melbourne's Muslim Leaders." Citeseer. https://citeseerx.ist.psu.edu/view doc/download?=10.1.1.994.2532&rep=rep1&type=pdf.

Ferguson, Kate. 2016. "Countering Violent Extremism through Media and Communication Strategies: A Review of the Evidence." Partnership for Conflict, Crime & Security Research. www.paccsresearch.org.uk/wp-con tent/uploads/2016/03/Countering-Violent-Extremism-Through-Media-and-Communication-Strategies-.pdf.

Fingas, J. 2019. "Australian Bill Could Imprison Social Network Execs over Violent Content." Engadget. www.engadget.com/2019-03-30-australia-laws-could-imprison-internet-execs.html.

Flores, Andrea, and Carrie James. 2013. "Morality and Ethics behind the Screen: Young People's Perspectives on Digital Life." *New Media & Society* 15 (6): 834–52.

Freedman, Lawrence Zelic. 1983. "Why Does Terrorism Terrorize?" *Terrorism* 6 (3): 389–401.

Frissen, Thomas. 2021. "Internet, the Great Radicalizer? Exploring Relationships between Seeking for Online Extremist Materials and Cognitive Radicalization in Young Adults." *Computers in Human Behavior* 114 (January): 106549.

Funk, Jeanne B., Heidi Bechtoldt Baldacci, Tracie Pasold, and Jennifer Baumgardner. 2004. "Violence Exposure in Real-Life, Video Games, Television, Movies, and the Internet: Is There Desensitization?" *Journal of Adolescence* 27 (1): 23–39.

Gadarian, Shana Kushner. 2010. "The Politics of Threat: How Terrorism News Shapes Foreign Policy Attitudes." *The Journal of Politics* 72 (2): 469–83.

2014. "Scary Pictures: How Terrorism Imagery Affects Voter Evaluations." *Political Communication* 31 (2): 282–302.

Gauntlett, David. 1998. "Ten Things Wrong with the Media 'Effects' Model." In *Approaches to Audiences: A Reader*, edited by Roger Dickinson, Ramaswani Harindranath, and Olga Linne, 120–30. London: Arnold.

Gibson, Kerry, and Susanna Trnka. 2020. "Young People's Priorities for Support on Social Media: 'It Takes Trust to Talk about These Issues.'" *Computers in Human Behavior* 102 (January): 238–47.

Gielen, Amy-Jane. 2019. "Countering Violent Extremism: A Realist Review for Assessing What Works, for Whom, in What Circumstances, and How?" *Terrorism and Political Violence* 31 (6): 1149–67.

Gill, Paul, Emily Corner, Maura Conway, Amy Thornton, Mia Bloom, and John Horgan. 2017. "Terrorist Use of the Internet by the Numbers: Quantifying Behaviors, Patterns, and Processes." *Criminology & Public Policy* 16 (1): 99–117.

Gillespie, Tarleton. 2018. *Custodians of the Internet: Platforms, Content Moderation, and the Hidden Decisions That Shape Social Media*. New Haven, CT: Yale University Press.

Grieve, Rachel, Michaelle Indian, Kate Witteveen, G. Anne Tolan, and Jessica Marrington. 2013. "Face-to-Face or Facebook: Can Social Connectedness Be Derived Online?" *Computers in Human Behavior* 29 (3): 604–9.

Grimmelmann, James. 2015. "The Virtues of Moderation." *Yale Journal of Law & Tech*nology 17: 42.

Grossman, Michele, Kristin Hadfield, Philip Jefferies, Vivian Gerrand, and Michael Ungar. 2020. "Youth Resilience to Violent Extremism: Development and Validation of the BRAVE Measure." *Terrorism and Political Violence*, January, 1–21.

Holbrook, Donald. 2015. "Designing and Applying an 'Extremist Media Index.'" *Perspectives on Terrorism* 9 (5): 57–68. www.universiteitleiden.nl/binaries/content/assets/customsites/perspectives-on-terrorism/2015/volume-5/6-designing-and-applying-an-%E2%80%98extremist-media-index%E2%80%99-57-by-donald-holbrook.pdf.

Hsee, Christopher K., and Bowen Ruan. 2016. "The Pandora Effect: The Power and Peril of Curiosity." *Psychological Science* 27 (5): 659–66.

Ilascu, Ionut. 2019. "New Zealand Mobile Carriers Block 8chan, 4chan, and LiveLeak." BleepingComputer. March 16, 2019. www.bleepingcomputer.com/news/security/new-zealand-mobile-carriers-block-8chan-4chan-and-liveleak/.

Iyer, Aarti, Matthew J. Hornsey, Eric J. Vanman, Sarah Esposo, and Shalini Ale. 2015. "Fight and Flight: Evidence of Aggressive Capitulation in the Face of Fear Messages from Terrorists: Responses to Terrorist Persuasion Appeals." *Political Psychology* 36 (6): 631–48.

Iyer, Aarti, and Julian Oldmeadow. 2006. "Picture This: Emotional and Political Responses to Photographs of the Kenneth Bigley Kidnapping." *European Journal of Social Psychology* 36 (5): 635–47.

James, Carrie, Katie Davis, Linda Charmaraman, Sara Konrath, Petr Slovak, Emily Weinstein, and Lana Yarosh. 2017. "Digital Life and Youth Well-Being, Social Connectedness, Empathy, and Narcissism." *Pediatrics* 140 (Suppl 2): S71–75.

Jenkins, Brian Michael. 1974. "Will Terrorists Go Nuclear?" RAND Corporation. www.rand.org/pubs/papers/P5541.html.

Johnston, Nicolas. 2019. "Christchurch Attack: The Dark Web of Terrorism as Entertainment." *The Interpreter*. March 19, 2019. www.lowyinstitute.org /the-interpreter/christchurch-attack-dark-web-terrorism-entertainment.

Jovanovic, Veljko, and Dragana Brdaric. 2012. "Did Curiosity Kill the Cat? Evidence from Subjective Well-Being in Adolescents." *Personality and Individual Differences* 52 (3): 380–4.

Kiper, J., and R. Sosis. 2015. "Why Terrorism Terrifies Us." https://doi.org/10 .4324/9781315772424-11.

Kirby, Aidan. 2007. "The London Bombers as 'Self-Starters': A Case Study in Indigenous Radicalization and the Emergence of Autonomous Cliques." *Studies in Conflict and Terrorism* 30 (5): 415–28.

Koehler, Daniel. 2017. *Understanding Deradicalization: Methods, Tools and Programs for Countering Violent Extremism*. London: Routledge.

Krieger, Tim, and Daniel Meierrieks. 2011. "What Causes Terrorism?" *Public Choice* 147 (1/2): 3–27.

Kruglanski, Arie W., Michele J. Gelfand, Jocelyn J. Bélanger, Anna Sheveland, Malkanthi Hetiarachchi, and Rohan Gunaratna. 2014. "The Psychology of Radicalization and Deradicalization: How Significance Quest Impacts Violent Extremism." *Political Psychology* 35: 69–93.

Lane, Daniel S., and Sonya Dal Cin. 2018. "Sharing beyond Slacktivism: The Effect of Socially Observable Prosocial Media Sharing on Subsequent Offline Helping Behavior." *Information, Communication and Society* 21 (11): 1523–40.

Laqueur, Walter. 2001. *A History of Terrorism*. New Brunswick, NJ: Transaction Publishers.

Lima, Lucas, Julio C.S. Reis, Philipe Melo, Fabricio Murai, Leandro Araujo, Pantelis Vikatos, and Fabricio Benevenuto. 2018. "Inside the Right-Leaning

Echo Chambers: Characterizing Gab, an Unmoderated Social System." In *2018 IEEE/ACM International Conference on Advances in Social Networks Analysis and Mining (ASONAM)*, 515–22.

Lindgren, Simon. 2017. *Digital Media and Society.* Los Angeles: Sage.

Litman, Jordan A., and Tiffany L. Jimerson. 2004. "The Measurement of Curiosity as a Feeling of Deprivation." *Journal of Personality Assessment* 82 (2): 147–57.

Livingstone, Sonia, Lucyna Kirwil, Cristina Ponte, and Elisabeth Staksrud. 2014. "In Their Own Words: What Bothers Children Online?" *European Journal of Disorders of Communication: The Journal of the College of Speech and Language Therapists,* London 29 (3): 271–88.

Lowe, D. 2019. "Christchurch Terrorist Attack, The Far-Right and Social Media: What Can We Learn?" *The New Jurist*, April. http://eprints .leedsbeckett.ac.uk/id/eprint/5822/.

Lupinacci, Ludmila. 2020. "'Absentmindedly Scrolling through Nothing': Liveness and Compulsory Continuous Connectedness in Social Media." *Media Culture & Society* 43 (2): 273–90. https://doi.org/10.1177 /0163443720939454.

Lyons, L. 2005. "What Frightens America's Youth?" 2005. https://news .gallup.com/poll/15439/what-frightens-americas-youth.aspx.

Malthaner, Stefan, and Peter Waldmann. 2014. "The Radical Milieu: Conceptualizing the Supportive Social Environment of Terrorist Groups." *Studies in Conflict and Terrorism* 37 (12): 979–98.

Marres, Noortje and Gerlitz, Carolin. 2018. "Social Media as Experiments in Sociality." In Marres, Noortje and Guggenheim, Michael and Wilkie, Alex, (eds.) *Inventing the Social*. Manchester, UK: Mattering Press, pp. 253-286

Matusitz, Jonathan. 2012. *Terrorism and Communication: A Critical Introduction.* 1st ed. Thousand Oaks, CA: Sage.

McHugh, Bridget Christine, Pamela Wisniewski, Rosson Mary Beth, and John M. Carroll. 2018. "When Social Media Traumatizes Teens: The Roles of Online Risk Exposure, Coping, and Post-Traumatic Stress." *Internet Research* 28 (5): 1169–88.

Meleagrou-Hitchens, Alexander, Audrey Alexander, and Nick Kaderbhai. 2017. "Literature Review The Impact of Digital Communications Technology on Radicalization and Recruitment." *International Affairs* 93 (5): 1233–49.

Midlarsky, Manus I. 2011. *Origins of Political Extremism: Mass Violence in the Twentieth Century and Beyond.* New York: Cambridge University Press.

Miles, Tim. 2015. "Halal? Ha! LOL: An Examination of Muslim Online Comedy as Counter-Narrative." *Comedy Studies* 6 (2): 167–78.

Möller-Leimkühler, Anne Maria. 2018. "Why Is Terrorism a Man's Business?" *CNS Spectrums* 23 (2): 119–28.

Mrug, Sylvie, Anjana Madan, Edwin W. Cook 3rd, and Rex A. Wright. 2015. "Emotional and Physiological Desensitization to Real-Life and Movie Violence." *Journal of Youth and Adolescence* 44 (5): 1092–1108.

Muniesa, F. 2018. "How to Spot the Behavioral Shibboleth and What to Do about It." *Inventing the Social*. https://core.ac.uk/download/pdf/159067873.pdf#page=195.

Murrell, Colleen. 2019. "The Christchurch Shooting Was Streamed Live, but Think Twice about Watching It." *ABC News*, March 15, 2019. www.abc.net.au/news/2019-03-15/christchurch-shooting-live-stream-think-twice-about-watching-it/10907258.

Nabi, Robin L. 2010. "The Case for Emphasizing Discrete Emotions in Communication Research." *Communication Monographs* 77 (2): 153–9.

Nacos, Brigitte L. 2016. *Terrorism and Counterterrorism*. 5th ed. New York: Routledge.

Nahon, Karine. 2015. "Where There Is Social Media There Is Politics." In *The Routledge Companion to Social Media and Politics*, 39–55. New York: Routledge.

Naji, Abu Bakr, William F. McCants, Combating Terrorism Center (U.S.), and John M. Olin Institute for Strategic Studies. 2006. "The Management of Savagery: The Most Critical Stage through Which the Umma Will Pass." Cambridge, MA: John M. Olin Institute for Strategic Studies, Harvard University.

Nasser-Eddine, Minerva, Bridget Garnham, Katerina Agostino, and Gilbert Caluya. 2011. "Countering Violent Extremism (CVE) Literature Review." https://apps.dtic.mil/sti/citations/ADA543686.

Nellis, Ashley Marie, and Joanne Savage. 2012. "Does Watching the News Affect Fear of Terrorism? The Importance of Media Exposure on Terrorism Fear." *Crime & Delinquency* 58 (5): 748–68.

Nesser, Petter, Anne Stenersen, and Emilie Oftedal. 2016. "Jihadi Terrorism in Europe: The IS-Effect." *Perspectives on Terrorism* 10 (6): 3–24.

Neumann, Peter R. 2013. "The Trouble with Radicalization." *International Affairs* 89 (4): 873–93.

New Zealand Classification Office. n.d. "Classification Decision: Christchurch Mosque Attack Livestream." Accessed February 26, 2021. www.classificationoffice.govt.nz/news/featured-classification-decisions/christchurch-mosque-attack-livestream/.

Niehoff, Esther, and Suzanne Oosterwijk. 2020. "To Know, to Feel, to Share? Exploring the Motives That Drive Curiosity for Negative Content." *Current Opinion in Behavioral Sciences* 35 (October): 56–61.

Norris, Pippa, Marion Just, and Montague Kern. 2003. *Framing Terrorism: The News Media, the Government and the Public*. London: Routledge.

Office of the eSafety Commissioner. "State of Play – Youth, Kids and Digital Dangers." 2018. Office of the eSafety Commissioner. www.esafety.gov.au /sites/default/files/2019-10/State%20of%20Play%20-%20Youth%20kids %20and%20digital%20dangers.pdf.

O'Hara, Kieron, and David Stevens. 2015. "Echo Chambers and Online Radicalism: Assessing the Internet's Complicity in Violent Extremism: The Internet's Complicity in Violent Extremism." *Policy and Internet* 7 (4). https://doi.org/10.1002/poi3.88.

Oxford English Dictionary. n.d. Oxford English Dictionary. Accessed March 17, 2021. www.oed.com/search?searchType=dictionary&q=Terror& _searchBtn=Search.

Pape, Robert A. 2003. "The Strategic Logic of Suicide Terrorism." *The American Political Science Review* 97 (3): 343–61.

Pascoe, C. J. 2011. "Resource and Risk: Youth Sexuality and New Media Use." *Sexuality Research & Social Policy: Journal of NSRC: SR & SP* 8 (1): 5–17.

Pfefferbaum, Betty, Thomas W. Seale, Edward N. Brandt Jr, Rose L. Pfefferbaum, Debby E. Doughty, and Scott M. Rainwater. 2003. "Media Exposure in Children One Hundred Miles from a Terrorist Bombing." *Annals of Clinical Psychiatry: Official Journal of the American Academy of Clinical Psychiatrists* 15 (1): 1–8.

Post, Jerrold M., Cody McGinnis, and Kristen Moody. 2014. "The Changing Face of Terrorism in the 21st Century: The Communications Revolution and the Virtual Community of Hatred." *Behavioral Sciences & the Law* 32 (3): 306–34.

Prot, Sara, and Douglas A. Gentile. 2014. "Chapter Eight – Applying Risk and Resilience Models to Predicting the Effects of Media Violence on Development." In *Advances in Child Development and Behavior*, edited by Janette B. Benson, 46: 215–44. Waltham, MA: Elsevier.

Rapoport, David C. 2001. "The Fourth Wave: September 11 in the History of Terrorism." *Current History* 100 (650): 419–24.

Reed, Alastair. 2018. "An Inconvenient Truth: Countering Terrorist Narratives – Fighting a Threat We Do Not Understand," July. https://icct .nl/publication/an-inconvenient-truth-countering-terrorist-narratives-fight ing-a-threat-we-do-not-understand/.

Rimé, Bernard. 2009. "Emotion Elicits the Social Sharing of Emotion: Theory and Empirical Review." *Emotion Review: Journal of the International Society for Research on Emotion* 1 (1): 60–85.

Ritzer, George, and Nathan Jurgenson. 2010. "Production, Consumption, Prosumption: The Nature of Capitalism in the Age of the Digital 'Prosumer.'" *Journal of Consumer Culture* 10 (1): 13–36.

Ryan, Tracii, Kelly A. Allen, Deleon L. Gray, and Dennis M. McInerney. 2017. "How Social Are Social Media? A Review of Online Social Behaviour and Connectedness." *Journal of Relationships Research* 8. E8. https://doi.org /10.1017/jrr.2017.13.

Sageman, Marc. 2008. *Leaderless Jihad: Terror Networks in the Twenty-First Century.* 1st Edition. Philadelphia: University of Pennsylvania Press.

2014. "The Stagnation in Terrorism Research." *Terrorism and Political Violence* 26 (4): 565–80.

Schlegel, Linda. 2019. "Chambers of Secrets? Cognitive Echo Chambers and the Role of Social Media in Facilitating Them. – VOX – Pol." VOX – Pol. October 2, 2019. www.voxpol.eu/chambers-of-secrets-cognitive-echo-chambers-and-the-role-of-social-media-in-facilitating-them/.

Schmid, Alex. 2005. "Terrorism as Psychological Warfare." *Democracy and Security* 1 (2): 137–46.

Schmid, Alex (ed.), 2013. *The Routledge Handbook of Terrorism Research.* Reprint edition. London: Routledge.

Schuurman, Bart, Lasse Lindekilde, Stefan Malthaner, Francis O'Connor, Paul Gill, and Noémie Bouhana. 2019. "End of the Lone Wolf: The Typology That Should Not Have Been." *Studies in Conflict and Terrorism* 42 (8): 771–8.

Scrivens, Ryan, Paul Gill, and Maura Conway. 2020. "The Role of the Internet in Facilitating Violent Extremism and Terrorism: Suggestions for Progressing Research." In *The Palgrave Handbook of International Cybercrime and Cyberdeviance*, edited by Thomas J. Holt and Adam M. Bossler, 1417–35. Cham, Switzerland: Springer International Publishing.

Scrivner, Coltan. 2020. "The Psychology of Morbid Curiosity." *Psychological Bulletin.* https://doi.org/10.31234/osf.io/xug34.

Shoshani, Anat, and Michelle Slone. 2008. "The Drama of Media Coverage of Terrorism: Emotional and Attitudinal Impact on the Audience." *Studies in Conflict and Terrorism* 31 (7): 627–40.

Sinclair, Samuel Justin, and Daniel Antonius. 2012. *The Psychology of Terrorism Fears.*Oxford: Oxford University Press. https://doi.org/10 .1093/acprof:oso/9780195388114.001.0001.

Solomon, Robert C., ed. 2008. "Myth Six: Two Flavours of Emotion, Positive and Negative." In *True to Our Feelings: What Emotions Are Really Telling Us*, 170–77. Oxford: Oxford University Press.

Staksrud, Elisabeth, and Sonia Livingstone. 2009. "Children and Online Risk." *Information, Communication and Society* 12 (3): 364–87.

Stenersen, Anne. 2008. "The Internet: A Virtual Training Camp?" *Terrorism and Political Violence* 20 (2): 215–33.

Stephan, Maria J. 2015. "Civil Resistance vs. ISIS." *Journal of Resistance Studies* 1 (2): 127–50.

Stetten, Moritz von. 2009. "Recent Literature on the Red Army Faction in Germany: A Critical Overview." *Critical Studies on Terrorism* 2 (3): 546–54.

Tang, Lijun. 2013. "The Politics of Flies: Mocking News in Chinese Cyberspace." *Chinese Journal of Communication* 6 (4): 482–96.

Third, Amanda, Delphine Bellerose, Juliano D. D. Oliveira, Girish Lala, and Georgina Theakstone. 2017. "Young and Online: Children's Perspectives on Life in the Digital Age." Sydney, Australia: Western Sydney University. www.end-violence.org/sites/default/files/paragraphs/down load/Young_and_Online_Children_perspectives_Dec_2017.pdf.

Thomas, Elise. 2020. "Manifestos, Memetic Mobilisation and the Chan Boards in the Christchurch Shooting." In *Counterterrorism Yearbook 2020*, edited by Isaac Kfir and John Coyne, 19–22. Canberra: Australian Strategic Policy Institute.

Urbis. 2018. "Evaluation of the COMPACT Program." Melbourne: Urbis PTY Ltd.

Vandoninck, Sofie, Leen d'Haenens, and Keith Roe. 2013. "Online Risks." *Journal of Children and Media* 7 (1): 60–78.

Vergani, Matteo. 2018. *How Is Terrorism Changing Us? Threat Perception and Political Attitudes in the Age of Terror.* Singapore: Palgrave Macmillan.

Von Behr, Ines, Anaïs Reding, Charlie Edwards, and Luke Gribbon, L. 2013. "Radicalisation in the Digital Era: The Use of the Internet in 15 Cases of Terrorism and Extremism." Rand. www.rand.org/content/dam/rand/pubs/ research_reports/RR400/RR453/RAND_RR453.pdf.

Vossen, Helen G. M., and Karin M. Fikkers. 2020. "The Mediating Role of Sympathy in the Relationship between Media Violence and Dutch Adolescents' Social Behaviors." *Journal of Children and Media*, September, 1–21. https://doi.org/10.1080/17482798.2020.1828118.

Waldek, Lise, Brian Ballsun-Stanton, and Julian Droogan. 2020. "After Christchurch: Mapping Online Right-Wing Extremists," November. https://doi.org/10.5281/zenodo.4071472.

Walden, Max. 2021. "Singaporean Teenager Arrested for Allegedly Planning Christchurch-Inspired Machete Attack on Mosques." *ABC News*, January 28, 2021. www.abc.net.au/news/2021-01-28/singapore-teen-arrested-planning-christchurch-inspired-attacks/13098244.

Warzel, Charlie. 2019. "The New Zealand Massacre Was Made to Go Viral." *The New York Times*, March 15, 2019. www.nytimes.com/2019/03/15/opinion/new-zealand-shooting.html.

Weimann, Gabriel, and Ari Ben Am. 2020. "Digital Dog Whistles: The New Online Language of Extremism." *International Journal of Security Studies* 2 (1): 1–24.

Weimann, Gabriel, and Bruce Hoffman. 2015. *Terrorism in Cyberspace: The Next Generation*. Washington, DC: Woodrow Wilson Center Press / Columbia University Press.

Weine, Stevan, John Horgan, Cheryl Robertson, Sana Loue, Amin Mohamed, and Sahra Noor. 2009. "Community and Family Approaches to Combating the Radicalization and Recruitment of Somali-American Youth and Young Adults: A Psychosocial Perspective." *Dynamics of Asymmetric Conflict* 2 (3): 181–200.

Williams, Michael J., and Steven M. Kleinman. 2014. "A Utilization-Focused Guide for Conducting Terrorism Risk Reduction Program Evaluations." *Behavioral Sciences of Terrorism and Political Aggression* 6 (2): 102–46.

Winner, Langdon. 1996. "Who Will We Be in Cyberspace?" *The Information Society* 12 (1): 63–72.

Winter, Charlie. 2015. "The Virtual 'Caliphate': Understanding Islamic State's Propaganda Strategy." 2015. www.stratcomcoe.org/charlie-winter-virtual-caliphate-understanding-islamic-states-propaganda-strategy.

Wolfowicz, Michael, Yael Litmanovitz, David Weisburd, and Badi Hasisi. 2020. "A Field-Wide Systematic Review and Meta-Analysis of Putative Risk and Protective Factors for Radicalization Outcomes." *Journal of Quantitative Criminology* 36 (3): 407–47.

Wright, Joanne. 1991. *Terrorist Propaganda: The Red Army Faction and the Provisional IRA, 1968–86*. London: Palgrave Macmillan.

Wright-Neville, David, and Debra Smith. 2009. "Political Rage: Terrorism and the Politics of Emotion." *Global Change, Peace & Security* 21 (1): 85–98.

Zekulin, Michael G. 2019. "The Internationalisation of White Nationalism: From Christchurch to El Paso and Beyond – Australian Institute of International Affairs." 2019. www.internationalaffairs.org.au/australianoutlook/the-internationalisation-of-white-nationalism-from-christchurch-to-el-paso-and-beyond/.

Zhang, Yin, and Louis Leung. 2015. "A Review of Social Networking Service (SNS) Research in Communication Journals from 2006 to 2011." *New Media & Society* 17 (7): 1007–24.

Cambridge Elements ≡

Histories of Emotions and the Senses

Jan Plamper

University of Limerick

Jan Plamper is Professor of History at the University of Limerick. His publications include *The History of Emotions: An Introduction* (Oxford, 2015); a multidisciplinary volume on fear; and articles on the sensory history of the Russian Revolution and on the history of soldiers' fears in World War One. He has also authored *The Stalin Cult: A Study in the Alchemy of Power* (Yale, 2012) and *Das neue Wir: Warum Migration dazugehört. Eine andere Geschichte der Deutschen* (S. Fischer, 2019).

About the Series

Born of the emotional and sensory 'turns,' *Elements in Histories of Emotions and the Senses* move one of the fastest-growing interdisciplinary fields forward. The series is aimed at scholars across the humanities, social sciences, and life sciences, embracing insights from a diverse range of disciplines, from neuroscience to art history and economics. Chronologically and regionally broad, encompassing global, transnational, and deep history, it concerns such topics as affect theory, intersensoriality, embodiment, human–animal relations, and distributed cognition.

Cambridge Elements ᗐ

Histories of Emotions and the Senses

Printed in the United States
by Baker & Taylor Publisher Services